In a world where budgets are shrinking, attention spans are shortening and resources are scarce - it's more urgent than ever to think differently, problem solve creatively and create something truly innovative. This work ensures innovation isn't just professed- it's actually practiced. Essential reading for anyone who's serious about changing the game to their advantage.

Friska Wirya

Top 50 change management thought leader,

Best-selling author of *The Future Fit Organisation*,

Indonesia.

Leaders at any level of an organisation striving to create a 'safe space' for innovation while sustaining their edge need to be ambidextrous themselves! Are you a leader undertaking that journey? Ugeng's book will give you that elevator ride you need!

Adrian Istani

Manager in a Big Four consulting firm,

United Kingdom.

This book is a must-read for anyone looking to drive meaningful innovation within their organisation. It provides clear, actionable insights and practical tools that can be applied immediately, making the complex world of innovation accessible to both new and seasoned leaders. Ugeng's approach to fostering creativity and strategic thinking in innovation are both inspiring and practical, offering a roadmap to creating a culture where new ideas can thrive. A game-changer for anyone serious about staying ahead in today's fast-paced market!

Nicodemus Winata

Partner & co-founder of Board Transformation and Excellence,

Former product manager at Fortune 300 companies in Chicago,

United States of America.

This book is a game-changer for leaders who want to revolutionise their organisations in today's world. Packed with actionable insights and real-world examples, this book is a must-read for anyone seeking to unlock their organisation's full potential in an era of rapid change.

Shiza Sheikh

Digital marketing manager in Dubai,

United Arab Emirates.

Innovation is the engine of significant advancement and long-term accomplishment; it is more than just a catchphrase. In a world that requires creativity and flexibility, your investigation of disruptive and sustaining

innovation provides priceless insights. By offering a road map for companies and individuals to rethink boundaries and embrace the future, it closes the gap between theory and practice. Anyone who wants to be at the forefront of influencing the future with vision and purpose should read this book.

Amolwan Nititham

Brand strategy executive,

Thailand.

Innovation is the key to standing out, whether as an individual, a company, a society, or on a global scale. This book provides a comprehensive exploration of the various types of innovation, shedding light on how value is created, delivered, and captured across different innovation models.

For anyone seeking growth—whether as an employee within a company or an entrepreneur in a startup—this book serves as an invaluable guide to success. I highly recommend it to forward-thinking minds eager to embrace the power of innovation.

Sanni Adedokun

Chief innovations and operations director,

Adedokun International Schools

(Best Private Senior Secondary School in Ogun State, Nigeria, 2024)

In today's world, innovation is all about harnessing the power of digital technology, with AI at the forefront. This book perfectly captures how we can embrace these transformative tools to stay ahead in the ever-evolving landscape. It's a must-read for anyone looking to future-proof their business and drive meaningful change. While leaders may think digital disruption is in the past, ai and the ensuing technological capabilities will surprise the unprepared.

Hugo Messer

Venture builder & impact investor,

The Netherlands.

Leading Innovation is a powerful guide for navigating the complexities of the corporate world. It masterfully combines practical strategies with deep insights into building resilience and fostering agility in leadership. The chapter 'The Characteristics of Innovation Leaders' resonated deeply with me. It breaks down complex ideas about leadership into actionable insights that are both practical and inspiring. The book provides a refreshing perspective on how resilience and agility can be cultivated in leaders, making it a must-read for anyone aiming to drive meaningful change in the corporate world. Kudos to Wijaya for creating a resource that's not only insightful but also engaging!

Nadeem Hussain,

Content and operations at a UK-based energy startup.

LEADING INNOVATION

Building Resilience and Agility in the Corporate World

UGENG WIJAYA

To my dearest wife, Dian, for your unwavering love, endless support, and belief in me—this journey is as much yours as it is mine.

To my precious baby boy, Belva; you are the light of my life and my greatest inspiration.

To my beloved parents, and my brother for your boundless guidance, wisdom, and unconditional love that have shaped me into who I am today.

With all my heart, always.

Acknowledgements

I want to sincerely thank Sam Khan, the incredible project manager, for this book. Your guidance, dedication, and attention to detail have been instrumental in bringing this project to life. I couldn't have done it without your support.

A big thank you also to Pantheon Publisher UK for believing in my work and helping to share it with readers around the world. Your efforts have made this journey truly special.

To everyone who contributed testimonials at the beginning of this book, your kind words and support mean the world to me. Thank you for your encouragement and belief in this work.

Contents

Foreword 1

Chapter 1: Introduction 3

    The Importance of Innovation in the Modern Business
Landscape 3

Chapter 2: Types of Innovation 13

Chapter 3: The Characteristics of Innovation Leaders 32

Chapter 4: Building a Culture of Innovation 47

    Creating a Safe Space for Innovation 47

Chapter 5: Innovation Strategy: Ensuring Successful
Innovation 58

    What Is Innovation Strategy? 58

Chapter 6: Overcoming Challenges in Leading Innovation 88

    Resistance to Change 88

    Budget Allocation 91

    Bureaucratic Barriers 93

    Success Stories of Companies Dealing With Innovation
Issues 95

Chapter 7: Innovation Management 102

    ISO Innovation Management 112

    The Innovation Process: Utilising a Design Thinking
Approach 121

Chapter 8: The Corporate Innovation Office, the Catalyst for Innovation 144

Appendix 172

Corporate Innovation Maturity Assessment 172

Foreword

What if I tell you that innovation isn't just a buzzword or a nice-to-have skill? It's the very thing that will determine whether you sink or swim in the fast-moving world we live in. In a time when change is the only constant, innovation is the fuel that powers success, without which, you'll be left behind. *Leading Innovation: A Guide for Innovation Leaders* isn't just another book on trends. It's a challenge for you to think bigger, push boundaries, and redefine what's possible in your world.

This isn't a book for people looking for easy answers. If you've picked it up, you're ready to dive deep into the heart of leadership and innovation. It's about taking risks, questioning what you know, and creating something that matters. This book will make you uncomfortable because true innovation always does. It's about turning the impossible into reality, and that takes more than just good ideas—it takes leadership, courage, and a willingness to fail and learn. Inside these pages, you'll discover how great innovators think, act, and lead. You'll learn what sets them apart: their vision to see what others can't, their creativity to solve problems in ways no one thought possible, and their resilience to keep going when things get tough. These are the qualities that will drive you to lead in a world where change is happening faster than ever.

But let's be clear: innovation isn't a walk in the park. It's a messy, unpredictable journey. You will face resistance, doubt, and failure. However, those who succeed are the ones who embrace these challenges, knowing that each obstacle is a stepping stone towards something greater. This book will arm you with the tools to navigate those rough waters, showing you how to spark new ideas, turn them into action, and drive real change.

In a world where innovation is the key to thriving, standing still is the same as moving backward. You'll need to be bold, brave, and unafraid to question the way things have always been done. This book is your invitation to do just that—to step up and lead the charge towards a future shaped by your ideas.

Innovation doesn't wait for anyone, and neither should you. Are you ready to lead? To challenge yourself? To create the future? If so, then this book is for you. I'd like to thank the visionaries, risk-takers, and creators whose ideas and experiences have shaped this work. And most of all, I'd like to thank you for daring to take the first step in your journey of transformation.

So, get ready to transform your leadership, your team, and your organisation. Let's make it happen!

Sincerely,

UG Wijaya,

Manchester, August 2024

Chapter 1: Introduction

The Importance of Innovation in the Modern Business Landscape

Today, innovation is no longer just a buzzword; it is the spearhead that determines the life or death of a business. Amid the acceleration of technology, changing consumer preferences, and increasingly fierce competition, companies that fail to innovate will be engulfed in irrelevance. This chapter provides insights into why innovation is the key in today's business world—not just to survive but to truly win the game.

At its core, innovation is about creating new value, whether in the form of ideas, products, services, or processes. But let us ponder this for a moment: is innovation limited to only groundbreaking discoveries that disrupt the market? Or does it encompass a deeper change in the culture and mindset within an organisation? Can innovation be present at every layer of an organisation, influencing how they respond to challenges and seize opportunities?

The 21st-century business landscape is dominated by volatility, uncertainty, complexity, and ambiguity. Traditional operating models that prioritise efficiency and risk avoidance are slowly being discarded. Conversely, agility, adaptability, and foresight are now the essential keys. And this is the essence of innovation—no longer a choice but an urgent necessity. A crucial question then arises: how can companies build a resilient culture of innovation to navigate the complexities of the modern world?

One of the reasons why innovation is so vital is the accelerating pace of technological change. New technologies not only transform industries but also create new business models and reshape customer expectations. Businesses that can adopt these technologies to innovate will achieve higher efficiencies, develop new products and services, and deliver better customer experiences. On the contrary, those who are slow to adapt will be swept away by nimbler competitors who truly understand how to meet the ever-evolving market demands.

Moreover, innovation is crucial for differentiation in a crowded marketplace. In an era where consumers are bombarded with choices, standing out requires more than just competitive pricing or superior quality; it demands uniqueness. Innovation enables businesses to differentiate themselves, offering unique value propositions that attract and retain customers. Whether through disruptive business models, novel marketing strategies, or groundbreaking products and services, innovation is a key differentiator that can set a company apart from its competitors.

In addition to driving growth and competitiveness, innovation plays a vital role in addressing some of the most pressing global challenges. From climate change and resource scarcity to health crises and social inequalities, businesses are increasingly expected to contribute to the solutions rather than being part of the problem.

Through sustainable innovation, companies can develop products and processes that not only generate economic value but also benefit society and the environment. This approach not only enhances a company's reputation and brand value but also ensures its long-term sustainability by aligning its operations with the broader goals of society.

Fostering an innovative culture is not without its challenges. It requires visionary leadership, a willingness to take calculated risks, and an environment that encourages experimentation and tolerates failure. Organisations must also invest in talent, technology, and processes that support innovation, creating an ecosystem that nurtures creativity and collaboration. Despite these challenges, the potential rewards of embracing innovation make it an essential endeavour for businesses aiming to excel in the modern era.

In conclusion, the importance of innovation in today's business landscape cannot be overstated. As the driving force behind growth, competitiveness, and sustainability, innovation is essential for businesses aiming to navigate the complexities of the 21st-century market. By embracing the concept, companies can not only survive but thrive, transforming challenges into opportunities and shaping the future of industries and society at large. The willingness to innovate will increasingly distinguish the leaders from the laggards, marking the path to success in an ever-evolving world.

What Is Innovation? Definitions and Concepts

In the realms of business, science, and technology, the terms 'innovation,' 'invention,' and 'creativity' are often used interchangeably, yet they encompass distinct concepts with unique characteristics and roles in the process of bringing new ideas to life. Understanding these differences is crucial for organisations aiming to foster a culture that nurtures new ideas and drives progress.

Creativity is the wellspring from which all novel ideas flow. It is the ability to transcend traditional ways of thinking or acting and to develop new and original ideas, methods, or objects. Creativity is the cognitive ability to see connections where others see none, to challenge the status quo, and to imagine the unimagined. It is the seed of both innovation and invention, providing the raw material, the initial spark, required to initiate change. While creativity is often associated with the arts, it is equally vital in scientific, business, and technological contexts, where new solutions to problems are constantly in demand.

Invention, on the other hand, is the creation of a new product, process, or method that has never existed before, coming into being as a tangible output of creativity. It is the act of bringing something entirely new into existence through the application of intellectual and creative prowess. Inventions can be revolutionary, significantly altering the way we live, work, or interact with the world around us. The light bulb, the telephone, and the internet are classic examples of inventions that have reshaped society. Invention requires a high degree of technical skill and knowledge, as it often involves the development of something that requires patents or copyrights for protection. However, an invention does not automatically lead to widespread use or commercial success; it is merely the first step in a long journey that may or may not culminate in innovation.

Innovation, then, is where creativity and invention find their true purpose and impact. It is the process of taking an idea, an invention, or a creative insight and transforming it into a product, service, or methodology that creates value or improves upon existing standards. Innovation is not limited to the creation of new products but also includes the improvement of existing products, services, processes, or ways of doing things. It is characterised by the successful implementation and adoption of new solutions that meet new requirements, unarticulated needs, or existing market needs in a novel way. Innovation can be incremental, representing small improvements on existing products or processes, or it can be radical, representing a significant breakthrough that dramatically changes the market or society.

The key difference between invention and innovation lies in their focus and outcome. Invention is about creating something new, while innovation is about creating new value or capturing value in a new way. An invention becomes an innovation when it is commercially exploited and adopted widely, changing the way people live, work, or conduct business. This distinction underscores the importance of not only generating new ideas but also effectively implementing and scaling them to achieve impact.

Furthermore, creativity is the underlying force that drives both invention and innovation. Without creativity, there would be no novel ideas to explore or develop into inventions or innovations. It is the starting point for all forms of value creation, making it a critical component in both the invention process and the broader context of innovation.

In conclusion, while creativity, invention, and innovation are closely related concepts, they occupy distinct roles in the process of creating and implementing new ideas. Creativity is the ability to generate novel and useful ideas; invention is the creation of something new that has never been made before; and innovation is the practical application of new inventions or creative ideas to improve products, processes, or services. Understanding these differences is crucial for leaders and organisations that aim to harness the power of new ideas to drive progress and achieve sustainable growth in an ever-changing world.

The Role of Innovation Leaders

In the dynamic theatre of modern business, innovation leaders emerge not merely as conductors of an orchestra but as alchemists, capable of transforming the base metals of raw ideas into the gold of market-disrupting innovations. The role of these visionary figures transcends traditional leadership, demanding a blend of creativity, strategic thinking, and an unerring capacity to navigate the unpredictable seas of change. As we delve into the essence of what makes an innovation leader truly effective, we must consider the nuanced complexities that define their journey and the impact they wield within the ecosystem of innovation.

Innovation leaders stand at the confluence of creativity and execution, where the ethereal potential of 'what could be' meets the concrete reality of 'what is.' They possess the unique ability to peer beyond the horizon, to see not just the possibilities inherent in new ideas but the pathways through which these ideas can be brought to fruition. Yet, one must ponder, is it the foresight to anticipate future trends that primarily distinguishes these leaders, or is it their capacity to mobilise resources and talent towards achieving a vision that has not yet been realised?

The landscape of innovation is fraught with challenges and uncertainties. For every groundbreaking product that reaches the market, countless others languish in the valley of abandoned prototypes and unrealised potential. Innovation leaders, therefore, must possess an indomitable resilience and an unwavering belief in the transformative power of unique ideas. They navigate the delicate balance between fostering a culture of creativity, where failure is seen not as a setback but as a stepping stone, and maintaining the strategic focus necessary to bring viable products to market. How do these leaders cultivate an environment that embraces risk yet remains anchored to the core mission of creating

9

value?

Central to the role of innovation leaders is the ability to inspire and galvanise their teams. Innovation, after all, is not the sole purview of the individual but the collective endeavour of many. These leaders excel in building diverse teams, recognising that groundbreaking ideas often emerge from the confluence of differing perspectives and disciplines. They are adept at facilitating collaboration, encouraging open communication, and ensuring that every team member feels empowered to contribute. But the question arises, in their quest to democratise the innovation process, how do innovation leaders ensure that the multitude of voices does not dilute the clarity of vision or impede decisive action?

Moreover, innovation leaders play a crucial role in bridging the gap between the present and the future. They are tasked with not only envisioning the future but also making it palpable and actionable in the present. This involves not just a deep understanding of current market trends and consumer behaviours but also an ability to anticipate the evolving needs and challenges that will shape the future landscape. They must then translate these insights into strategic initiatives that propel their organisations forward, often in directions that diverge from established norms and practices. This visionary approach raises an intriguing consideration: in their pursuit of the future, how do innovation leaders ensure that they do not stray too far from the realms of feasibility, risking the alienation of stakeholders and consumers who may not yet be ready to embrace radical change?

In navigating these complexities, innovation leaders embody the paradoxical blend of dreamer and pragmatist. They are the architects of the future yet grounded in the realities of business and market dynamics. Their role is not just to invent new products or services but to reinvent the very paradigms through which we understand and engage with the world.

Ultimately, the true measure of an innovation leader's success lies not in the number of patents they hold or the accolades they receive but in their ability to cultivate a culture of continuous renewal and adaptation within their organisations. By fostering an environment where creativity, risk-taking, and resilience are celebrated, they pave the way for their teams to become the vanguards of progress, unlocking new frontiers of value creation and propelling their organisations into a future that is constantly being redefined.

In conclusion, the role of innovation leaders in today's business environment is both critical and multifaceted. They are the catalysts for change, the visionaries who dare to imagine a different future, and the strategists who plot the course to get there. Through their leadership, organisations can transcend the ordinary, embracing the extraordinary potential of innovation to redefine industries and impact society. As we reflect on the transformative journey of innovation, we are compelled to ask: what are the qualities that define a truly great innovation leader, and how can we cultivate these qualities within ourselves and others? It is a question that invites us to explore the depths of our own potential to lead and innovate in an ever-changing world.

Chapter 2: Types of Innovation

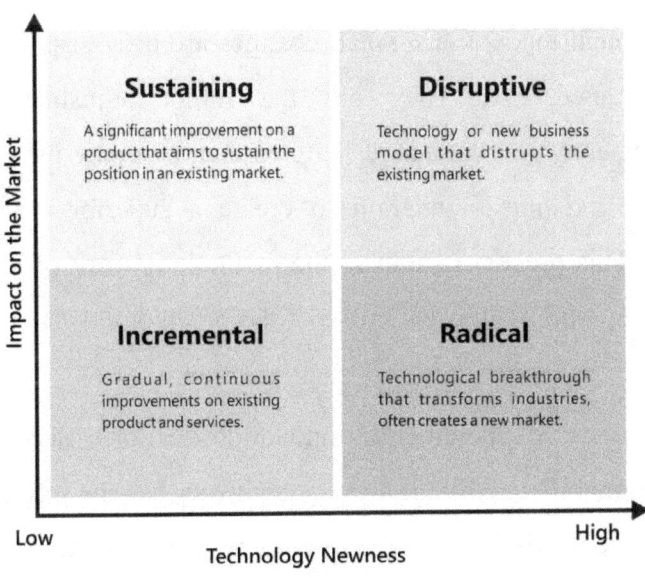

Source: freshconsulting.com

Incremental Innovation

In the world of innovation, where the bold and the revolutionary often steal the spotlight, there lies a subtle yet profoundly impactful thread known as incremental innovation. This type of innovation, characterised by its step-by-step improvements to existing products, services, or processes, may not command the headlines like its radical counterparts, but its cumulative effect on the world of business and beyond is undeniable. Incremental innovation is the unsung hero of progress, the steady hand that guides the continuous enhancement of our daily lives.

At its core, incremental innovation is about refinement. It is the art of taking something good and making it better, one small step at a time. Unlike the seismic shifts brought about by radical or breakthrough innovations, small changes are often less visible to the untrained eye. They are the minor adjustments, the enhancements, and the added features that, piece by piece, build upon the existing foundation to create a superior product or service. This process is akin to the meticulous work of a master craftsman, who, with each stroke of the brush or chisel, enhances the beauty and functionality of their creation.

The power of incremental innovation lies in its accessibility and sustainability. While not every company has the resources or the appetite for risk to pursue groundbreaking innovations, almost all can adopt the process of integrating minor adjustments. This democratisation of innovation allows organisations of all sizes to participate in the process of shaping the future, fostering a culture of continuous improvement that can lead to significant advancements over time.

Moreover, incremental innovation plays a crucial role in maintaining competitiveness in a fast-paced market. In industries where technological advancements and consumer preferences evolve at breakneck speed, the ability to swiftly adapt and refine existing offerings can be a critical factor in staying ahead of the curve. By continuously enhancing their products or services, companies can keep their offerings relevant and appealing to consumers, ensuring a steady stream of revenue and sustained market presence.

The beauty of incremental innovation also lies in its compound effect. While each improvement may seem modest in isolation, the cumulative impact of these changes over time can be transformative. Just as the compounding of interest can turn modest savings into a substantial nest egg, the continuous application of subtle improvements can lead to significant enhancements in product quality, efficiency, and user satisfaction. This process not only extends the lifecycle of a product or service but also can create a formidable barrier to entry for competitors, solidifying a company's market position.

However, the pursuit of incremental innovation is not without its challenges. It requires a keen eye for detail, a deep understanding of customer needs, and a commitment to continuous learning and adaptation. Organisations must foster a culture that encourages experimentation and values feedback, allowing for the free flow of ideas and the willingness to implement small changes that can lead to big results. This environment should celebrate incremental gains and recognise the long-term value they bring rather than solely focusing on the allure of more dramatic innovations.

Furthermore, incremental innovation demands a strategic approach to resource allocation and project management. Companies must carefully balance the need for ongoing improvements with the risk of overextending themselves or losing focus on their core offerings. This balancing act is crucial for ensuring that the process drives growth without diluting the brand or overwhelming the organisation with too many concurrent initiatives.

The domain of incremental innovation encompasses a compelling narrative about the evolution of the smartphone, a ubiquitous technology in contemporary society. This trajectory epitomises the essence of incremental innovation, demonstrating how minor, successive improvements can collectively transform a product and redefine an entire industry.

The inception of the smartphone itself was a revolutionary leap, combining the functionality of a mobile phone and a personal digital assistant (PDA). However, the true marvel lies in its evolution, a testament to the power of incremental innovation. Each new generation of smartphones has brought with it refinements and enhancements that, while perhaps modest individually, have significantly elevated the user experience and expanded the device's capabilities over time.

Consider the incremental improvements in screen technology. The transition from the early resistive touchscreens, which required pressure to register a touch, to the capacitive touchscreens of modern smartphones has made the devices more intuitive and user-friendly. Each iteration of screen technology—whether it be improvements in resolution, durability, or responsiveness—has contributed to making the smartphone more engaging and versatile.

Battery life is another domain where incremental innovation has had a profound impact. Early smartphones were often criticised for their short battery lives, limiting their utility and appeal. Through a series of small but significant advancements in battery technology, energy efficiency, and software optimisation, manufacturers have successfully extended the operational life of smartphones, enhancing their convenience and attractiveness to users.

The camera technology incorporated into smartphones also illustrates the power of incremental innovation. From the introduction of the first camera phones with their grainy, low-resolution images to the sophisticated multi-lens systems found in today's devices capable of capturing high-definition photos and videos, the gradual improvements have significantly enriched the user experience. These enhancements have not only improved the quality of the visuals captured but have also introduced features such as optical image stabilisation, low-light photography, and advanced editing capabilities, effectively turning the smartphone into a substitute for a high-end camera for many users.

Moreover, the continuous refinement of user interfaces (UI) and operating systems (OS) exemplifies incremental innovation's role in enhancing usability and functionality. Each update brings with it enhancements—smoother navigation, more intuitive layouts, increased customisation options, and improved security features—that make smartphones more personal, secure, and easier to use.

These examples of incremental innovation in smartphones highlight how small, ongoing changes can accumulate to produce significant overall improvements. This process not only keeps the product at the cutting edge of technology but also continually redefines user expectations and experiences. The smartphone's evolution underscores the importance of looking beyond the allure of groundbreaking inventions and recognising the transformative potential of making consistent, incremental advancements. Through this lens, we can appreciate how the commitment to gradual improvement has not only shaped the trajectory of the industry but has also offered valuable insights into the enduring impact of incremental innovation across all sectors.

In conclusion, incremental innovation represents a vital component of the innovation ecosystem. It is the steady force that drives continuous improvement, enhancing our lives in ways both small and significant. Through the persistent and thoughtful application of incremental changes, companies can not only refine their offerings but also foster a culture of innovation that propels them forward in a competitive landscape. The journey of incremental innovation may not always be glamorous, but its impact is undeniable, proving that even the smallest steps can lead to monumental achievements. As we navigate the complexities of the modern world, let us not underestimate the power of incremental innovation to shape the future, one step at a time.

Sustaining Innovation

In the intricate dance of progress where innovation leads, two subtle yet distinct steps—incremental and sustaining innovation—mark the rhythm of advancement in the business world. While both play crucial roles in propelling industries forward, understanding their nuances is crucial for any leader looking to navigate the complexities of growth and competitiveness. Incremental innovation, as the name suggests, involves making small, continuous improvements to products, services, or processes. It's about refining what already exists, often focusing on efficiency, cost reduction, or minor feature enhancements. Sustaining innovation, on the other hand, takes a step deeper, aiming not just to improve but to significantly enhance or upgrade existing products and services to meet the evolving needs of current customers. It's the pursuit of substantial, meaningful changes that sustain a company's relevance and ensure its offerings remain at the forefront of consumer demand.

The distinction between incremental and sustaining innovation can be likened to the difference between maintaining a garden and cultivating it to yield richer, more varied produce. Incremental innovation is the regular tending—watering, weeding, and pruning—that keeps the garden healthy but fundamentally unchanged. Sustaining innovation, meanwhile, involves introducing new varieties of plants or advanced cultivation techniques that significantly enhance the garden's bounty. Both are essential for the garden's growth and well-being, but they serve different purposes in its lifecycle.

Sustaining innovation requires a visionary approach, one that looks beyond the surface to identify and implement changes that will significantly impact and enhance the user experience. It is rooted in a deep understanding of customer needs, technological advancements, and market dynamics. This type of innovation asks, "How can we take what we have and significantly improve it to better serve our customers?" It's not about reinvention but rather about pushing the boundaries of what's already there to achieve greater value and performance.

The challenge and beauty of sustaining innovation lie in its potential to significantly impact a company's competitive edge without venturing into the unknown territories of market creation that characterise disruptive innovation. It is a strategic choice that focuses on strengthening and deepening the value proposition to existing customers, thereby reinforcing brand loyalty and market position. Companies that excel in sustaining innovation listen intently to their customer base, anticipate their evolving needs, and apply advanced technologies and processes to meet those needs in superior ways.

However, navigating the path of sustaining innovation is not without its hurdles. It demands a delicate balance between the current operational success and the future strategic vision. Organisations must cultivate an environment where bold ideas are encouraged and the status quo is regularly challenged, yet without losing sight of their core mission and capabilities. It requires a culture where risk is managed judiciously, and failures are seen as stepping stones to greater achievements.

Moreover, sustaining innovation calls for leadership that is both courageous and insightful. Leaders must be adept at reading the subtle shifts in consumer behaviour and technological trends, translating these insights into actionable innovation strategies. They must foster a culture of agility, where the organisation can pivot and adapt as new information and opportunities arise. This kind of leadership ensures that sustaining innovation is not just an occasional initiative but a continuous, integral part of the organisation's DNA.

In the realm of medical technology, the evolution of magnetic resonance imaging (MRI) and computed tomography (CT) scanners epitomises the essence of sustaining innovation. These technologies, central to modern diagnostic medicine, have undergone a series of enhancements that, while incremental, have collectively revolutionised patient care. This narrative unfolds not as a sudden leap into the unknown but as a meticulous journey of refinement, where each step brings us closer to a future of unparalleled precision in medical diagnostics.

Initially, the advent of MRI and CT scanning technologies marked a radical shift in medical capabilities, offering a non-invasive glimpse into the human body's inner workings. However, the true marvel of these technologies lies in their sustained evolution. Incremental improvements have systematically addressed their limitations, expanding their utility, improving their accuracy, and making them more accessible to patients worldwide.

One of the pivotal areas of sustaining innovation in MRI and CT technology is image quality. Early iterations, though groundbreaking, were limited by lower resolution, longer scan times, and significant challenges in distinguishing between tissues. Through continuous research and development, there have been significant advancements in imaging techniques and scanner hardware. Enhanced algorithms for image processing, higher magnet strengths for MRI, and more sophisticated X-ray sources for CT have all led to crisper, more detailed images. These improvements have not only facilitated more accurate diagnoses but have also expanded the range of conditions that can be detected and studied, from early-stage cancers to minute vascular abnormalities.

Another critical area of advancement is the reduction in scan time and increased patient comfort. Initially, both MRI and CT scans could be time-consuming and, in the case of MRI, particularly claustrophobic for patients. Sustaining innovations have focussed on making these machines faster and more patient-friendly. For instance, developments in faster imaging sequences for MRIs and more efficient scanning paths for CTs have significantly reduced the time patients spend in the scanner. Moreover, efforts to make the machines quieter and more comfortable have greatly improved the patient experience, reducing anxiety and movement artifacts, which, in turn, enhances image quality.

Radiation exposure, particularly in the case of CT scans, has been a significant concern. Sustaining innovation has led to the development of low-dose CT technologies that minimise radiation exposure without compromising image quality. This advancement represents a critical stride forward in patient safety, making routine screenings and follow-up scans less risky for patients.

Furthermore, the integration of advanced software and artificial intelligence (AI) into MRI and CT systems exemplifies how sustaining innovation can transform the user experience for both patients and healthcare providers. AI-driven analysis can help in the faster interpretation of scans, identify patterns that may be missed by the human eye, and predict patient outcomes, thereby supporting more personalised and effective treatment plans.

The evolution of MRI and CT scanners through the lens of sustaining innovation highlights a broader narrative of progress driven by the deliberate and thoughtful enhancement of existing technologies. Each incremental improvement—whether aimed at image quality, patient comfort, safety, or diagnostic accuracy—

builds upon the last, pushing the boundaries of what is possible in medical diagnostics.

This journey underscores the power of sustaining innovation not merely as a strategy for maintaining relevance but as a commitment to pushing the envelope of patient care. The continuous evolution of MRI and CT technologies stands as a testament to the medical community's relentless pursuit of better, safer, and more precise diagnostic tools. It illustrates that in the quest for innovation, sometimes the most groundbreaking advancements are those that unfold incrementally, shaping the future one enhancement at a time.

In conclusion, sustaining innovation represents a powerful strategy for companies seeking to maintain and enhance their market relevance. It is a testament to the understanding that in the fast-paced world of business, standing still is not an option. The commitment to making substantial, meaningful improvements to existing products and services is what enables companies to thrive in an ever-evolving landscape. Through the lens of sustaining innovation, organisations can see beyond the horizon, anticipating and meeting the needs of their customers in ways that are both significant and transformative. This journey, while challenging, is replete with opportunities for growth, differentiation, and lasting impact, marking the path for those who aim to lead rather than follow in the march of progress.

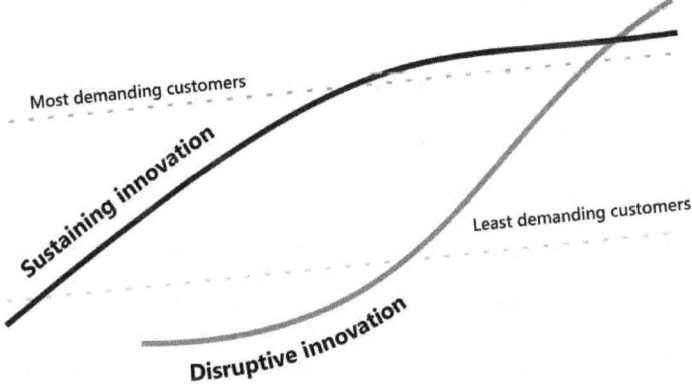

Most demanding customers

Sustaining innovation

Least demanding customers

Disruptive innovation

Source: viima.com

Disruptive Innovation

In the tapestry of innovation that adorns the halls of progress, disruptive innovation emerges as one of the most striking threads, bold and transformative, reshaping industries and society at their core. Unlike its counterparts—incremental, sustaining, and radical innovations—disruptive innovation occupies a unique space, challenging established markets and introducing new ways to address needs previously overlooked. It represents advancements that dramatically alter how we understand, use, and interact with products, services, or technologies, redefining industries and often leading to entirely new market categories.

Disruptive innovation often stems from an understanding of unmet needs or by combining disparate ideas in a way that solves a problem in a fundamentally new way. This type of innovation is the product of visionary thinking, relentless curiosity, and a willingness to explore beyond conventional boundaries. The solutions don't simply improve upon existing products—they leap forward, offering significant advantages over current options and sometimes making established solutions obsolete. They have the power to redefine consumer expectations, reshape industries, and open up new avenues for growth and exploration.

Consider the advent of the smartphone as an example of disruptive innovation. It was not merely an incremental improvement on the mobile phone; instead, it introduced a new paradigm in communication technology, merging the functionalities of a phone, a camera, and a computer into a single, portable device. This disruption didn't just upgrade an existing product—it created a new category of personal technology that has since become integral to daily life, reshaping how we communicate, access information, and interact with the world.

The path to disruptive innovation is fraught with challenges and uncertainties, requiring a delicate balance between creativity and discipline, intuition and analysis. Innovators must navigate uncharted territory, armed with a conviction in their vision and a willingness to embrace failure as part of the journey. This path often involves significant investment—not only financially but in terms of time, effort, and resilience. The risks are high, but the rewards, both economically and socially, can be monumental.

Moreover, disruptive innovations require an ecosystem that fosters and sustains creative thinking and experimentation. This ecosystem includes a supportive culture that encourages risk-taking, access to resources and expertise to refine ideas, and a regulatory environment that incentivises innovation. Collaborations between academia, industry, and government can further catalyse disruptive innovations by pooling diverse perspectives and capabilities.

Disruptive innovation's impact extends beyond the immediate benefits of a new product or service. It often sets off a ripple effect, sparking further innovations and inspiring new ways of thinking. Competitors are compelled to respond, either by adapting to the new technology or by pursuing further innovation, creating a cycle of continuous advancement. Disruptive innovations can also tackle global challenges—such as climate change, health crises, and social inequality—by providing novel solutions that surpass traditional approaches.

However, disruptive innovation is not without its downsides. It can bring about ethical and societal questions that require thoughtful consideration. Disruptions can lead to displacement within industries, obsolescence of skills, and broader societal shifts. Addressing these challenges demands a mindful approach to innovation, one that seeks to maximise benefits for society while mitigating negative impacts.

Imagine you're walking through a well-worn forest path, representing the familiar world with all its established norms and routines. Suddenly, you stumble upon a clearing bathed in sunlight, revealing a new path with unprecedented possibilities. This is the essence of disruptive innovation: the discovery of a new path that changes not only the way we navigate the world but the very landscape itself.

The story of the first digital camera illustrates disruptive innovation well. In a world accustomed to film photography, where one waited a day to see captured moments, the digital camera was like finding that sunlit clearing. It didn't just improve photography; it transformed the profession, allowing people to instantly capture and share images, democratising photography for millions and spawning new industries and hobbies.

The digital camera's disruptive impact went beyond photography, influencing communication, memory, and even culture. It paved the way for smartphones, embedding photography into daily communication and making images as ubiquitous as words.

The journey towards disruptive innovation may be complex and fraught with uncertainty, but it is also thrilling and deeply rewarding. It requires vision, resilience, and an ecosystem that nurtures groundbreaking ideas. As we look to the future, disruptive innovations will continue to drive economic growth, social progress, and solutions to humanity's greatest challenges. These innovations are a testament to human creativity, continually reshaping the world and expanding what is possible.

Radical Innovation

Radical innovation represents a transformative leap in technology or concepts, often creating new markets or industries or reshaping existing ones. Unlike incremental improvements, radical innovation introduces groundbreaking changes that shift the way we perceive or use technology, products, or services. Such innovations aren't just refinements but often require the development of entirely new knowledge bases and the adoption of novel technologies. Radical innovations are also high-stakes due to their unpredictability, often involving high risk, but their success can revolutionise industries and lead to long-term competitive advantages.

The impact of radical innovation lies in its potential to open doors to new possibilities that previously seemed impossible. For example, the advent of the internet drastically changed the way people communicate, work, and access information. Similarly, the development of artificial intelligence has paved the way for machines capable of tasks once exclusive to humans, such as image recognition, speech processing, and complex data analysis. Radical innovation usually demands significant investment in research and development, as it often involves pushing the boundaries of existing technologies or creating entirely new ones.

Radical innovation generally requires organisational support and a culture willing to embrace change and experimentation. Companies engaging in radical innovation typically invest time and resources to foster creativity and challenge conventional thinking, as these elements are crucial for breakthrough discoveries. For instance, the early days of electric vehicles required substantial R&D investments in battery technology, manufacturing processes, and infrastructure development. Organisations that manage to successfully cultivate these radical innovations tend to gain a competitive edge, as they can capitalise on the novelty and first-mover advantages.

However, radical innovation differs significantly from disruptive innovation, even though both may result in substantial changes to industries. Disruptive innovation, a term popularised by Clayton Christensen, refers to innovations that initially target a niche or underserved segment of the market, often with a product or service that is simpler, cheaper, or more accessible than existing offerings. Over time, disruptive innovations improve and start to appeal to mainstream customers, eventually replacing or reshaping incumbents' market shares. A classic example of disruptive innovation is the rise of digital photography, which began with lower quality than film but eventually evolved to match and surpass it, rendering film photography nearly obsolete.

In contrast, radical innovation is not necessarily focussed on entering an underserved market but on introducing completely new technologies or concepts that redefine an industry or create a new one. Radical innovation can be highly impactful but doesn't always follow the same trajectory as disruptive innovation in terms of market entry. Instead, it often seeks to introduce breakthroughs that transform industries from the top down, appealing to all market segments. While both types of innovation drive change, radical innovation typically reshapes the technological landscape more broadly, whereas disruptive innovation focuses on changing business models and market structures.

Chapter 3: The Characteristics of Innovation Leaders

Visionary Leader

In the world of innovation, a visionary leader is one who not only sees what is in front of him but can also project a much bigger future. Steve Jobs, with his incredible intelligence, is a perfect example of a leader who sees the world not as it is now but as how it can become better, more sophisticated, and more connected.

In 1983, Steve Jobs introduced Lisa, a personal computer that was revolutionary for the time. But more than just a product, Lisa represents Jobs' vision of what could be an ideal personal computer device. At that time, he envisioned a computer that was not just a work tool but something that could be carried everywhere, even seen as something light and comfortable like a book. The computer should be intuitive and elegant as if it could be a part of everyday life—a device that can be carried like a notebook, not a huge machine that limits the user's mobility.

Of course, in 1983, Jobs' vision for a computer that could be carried everywhere was too ambitious. Lisa never really achieved it. However, that doesn't mean the vision is over. Jobs had the ability to look further ahead, and even though Lisa didn't achieve her goals, a bigger vision continued to develop in his mind.

Year after year, Jobs continued to challenge the boundaries of technology and set Apple to create devices that truly changed the way we work, communicate, and live. In 2008, more than 25 years after Lisa, Jobs unveiled the MacBook Air. This product not only fulfilled Jobs' dream of a lighter and more portable computer but even exceeded it. The MacBook Air is not just a device like a book, but even better. With its ultra-thin thickness and charming design, MacBook Air can be put in an envelope. This is an innovation that not only fulfils Jobs' dream but exceeds what expectations might have been achieved at first.

As Steve Jobs once said, "Innovation differentiates between leaders and followers." These words describe how he did not just follow trends but created a completely new future. He saw the world not as what it was there but as it could be, even if others couldn't imagine it yet. With the MacBook Air, Steve Jobs didn't just realise his vision for a computer that could fit in an envelope— he revolutionised the design of technology devices that were sleeker and more portable than ever before.

In conclusion, Steve Jobs is a classic example of a visionary leader. He sees the future not as a distant thing but as an opportunity that can be realised through dedication, courage, and the ability to challenge existing boundaries. Jobs' vision not only changed Apple but the tech world as a whole, teaching us that true innovation comes when we look beyond existing boundaries and shape a better future.

Dare to Take Risks

In the world of innovation, the courage to take risks is the fuel that allows big ideas to explode into reality. Without risk, there will be no breakthrough—only comfort zones that limit the limits of our achievements. True innovation leaders know that to achieve big things, they must step out of their comfort zone, face uncertainty, and be willing to fail. Without this courage, we will just continue to spin in place, stuck in old habits.

Taking risks does not mean acting recklessly or rashly. Rather, it is about careful calculation and readiness to face the consequences of the choices made. Leaders who dare to take risks have the courage to see opportunities where others only see obstacles. They realise that behind every risk is great potential for growth and change that leads to great success.

Elon Musk is a perfect example of a leader who dares to take risks. Through the company SpaceX, which he founded in 2002, Musk is not only trying to compete with large space agencies such as NASA, but he is also changing the paradigm of the space industry that was previously dominated by governments and large corporations.

At the time SpaceX first launched its rockets, many people doubted the ability of private companies to succeed in the space industry. Many consider the cost and technical complexity of spaceflight to be an impossible challenge for a relatively small private company. However, Musk doesn't just see the challenge—

he sees a huge opportunity to democratise space exploration, lower the cost of space travel, and even open up possibilities for human life on Mars.

Musk's courage to take risks was very evident when SpaceX invested a large amount of money to develop reusable rockets, which were considered almost impossible to realise. Many people are sceptical, doubting the ability of this technology to work, and even consider it a futile experiment. But he dared to go further by accepting the fact that failure is part of the process—and he is ready to face it. In fact, after several major failures in rocket launches, Musk has persevered and continues to innovate.

The courage to continue investing in seemingly impossible technologies and ideas yields incredible results. SpaceX has successfully developed a Falcon 9 rocket that can return to Earth after launch and be reused, which dramatically reduces the cost of space launches. This success not only demonstrated the potential of the technology but also shook up the space industry, paving the way for private companies to engage in space exploration more actively.

As Musk once said, "If something is important enough, even if the chance of success is only 10%, you should do it anyway." These words describe his philosophy that the greatest success comes from the courage to take big steps, even when the odds seem small. Musk's courage to take risks not only changed SpaceX but also changed the entire space industry, opening new possibilities for future space exploration and commercialisation.

In conclusion, innovation leaders are those who are not afraid to face the uncertainty and difficulties that come with pursuing big ideas. They see failure not as the end but as a step on the road to success. Elon Musk shows us that only by taking big risks can we achieve incredible results, create impactful change, and inspire the world to think bigger, farther, and bolder.

Collaborative

In the world of innovation leadership, the spirit of collaboration stands as an irreplaceable foundation, a game-changing element. Collaboration is not just about working together but the art of combining diverse talents, experiences, and views into a harmonious symphony of innovation. It's about realising that the best ideas often come at the intersection of different perspectives when different minds come together to solve complex puzzles. Collaboration requires leaders who are able to unite teams with a common vision but also value every voice heard and valued.

Collaboration is not just about sharing tasks but about creating a culture that encourages the exchange of ideas, where failure is not a setback but a step towards discovery. Leadership that prioritises collaboration paves the way for the achievement of extraordinary innovations, which may not be achieved by individual efforts. Collaboration relies on collective intelligence to explore new possibilities and achieve previously unimaginable breakthroughs.

Jensen Huang, founder and CEO of NVIDIA, is a clear example of the power of collaboration in action. Under his leadership, NVIDIA, which was once just a small startup focussed on graphics processing units (GPUs) for games, has transformed into a leading tech giant in the fields of artificial intelligence (AI), deep learning, and autonomous vehicles. This monumental change is not only the result of Huang's vision alone but is also a tangible testament to the collaborative culture he built at NVIDIA.

Initially, GPUs were designed to render images in video games. However, Huang and his team realised that the parallel processing capabilities of GPUs have potential that goes far beyond just gaming. They saw opportunities that others couldn't see, and that was the beginning of NVIDIA's journey into the world of AI, a field that requires technical expertise as well as creative thinking and cross-disciplinary collaboration.

However, this transition from gaming to AI has not been an easy one. It takes researchers from different fields—computer science, neuroscience, and mathematics—to come together, share knowledge, and figure out how GPUs can be used for deep learning. Huang built an environment where this cross-disciplinary collaboration was not only encouraged but celebrated. He understands that to lead in the world of AI, NVIDIA must leverage the collective intelligence of its entire team, digging into a wide range of expertise to innovate and solve problems.

One of NVIDIA's major breakthroughs under Huang's

leadership was the development of CUDA, a parallel computing platform and application programming interface (API) model. CUDA makes it easy for developers to use general-purpose processing GPUs (GPGPUs). This breakthrough is crucial in accelerating the adoption of GPU computing in AI, accelerating tasks such as machine learning algorithms and deep learning.

Huang's approach to leadership—which emphasises collaboration, building cross-functional teams, and encouraging open communication—has been key to NVIDIA's success. By creating a culture where employees are motivated to collaborate, share ideas, and push boundaries, the company remains at the forefront of technological innovation.

NVIDIA's journey under Jensen Huang's leadership is a vivid example of how collaboration in innovation leadership can lead to world-changing breakthroughs. This shows that when a leader is able to bring people together, bridge disciplines, and combine talents towards a common goal, the potential to innovate becomes limitless. Huang's belief in the power of collaboration not only takes his organisation to new markets but also redefines the role of GPUs and sets new standards in the tech industry.

In the narrative of innovation leadership, collaboration emerges as a fundamental chapter, reminding us that the path to extraordinary achievement is often built with joint effort and collective wisdom. Jensen Huang's story with NVIDIA shows just how powerful collaboration can be, confirming that when diverse minds work together, united by a visionary leader, they can redefine the boundaries of technology and open up new horizons for the world.

Adaptive

Jeff Bezos is a very apt example of adaptability in leadership. As the founder of Amazon, Bezos shows how a leader must be ready to change strategies, focuses, and even business models in order to survive and thrive in a world full of uncertainty and rapid change.

From the beginning, Bezos has shown its ability to adapt to changing markets and consumer needs. Started in 1994, Amazon was originally designed as an online bookstore. At that time, many people doubted the internet-based business model, and many believed that the online market would never be able to compete with physical stores. However, Bezos has a vision far ahead that the internet will change the way people shop. When the online bookstore was first launched, no one expected that Amazon would evolve into the global e-commerce giant that exists today.

However, Bezos' adaptability does not stop there. In the midst of its initial success as an online bookstore, it quickly recognised that in order to expand further, Amazon needed to transform and offer more than just books. In 1998, Amazon began adding other product categories, such as electronics and other consumer goods. This is a bold move that expands Amazon into a giant online marketplace that is much larger than a bookstore.

Bezos is not only adapting to product developments, but also to technology and changing consumer behaviour. One of the best examples of its adaptability was when he decided to develop Amazon Web Services (AWS) in 2006. At the time, cloud computing services were not commonplace, and many doubted whether it would be a profitable business model. However, Bezos sees a huge opportunity to provide cloud infrastructure to other companies that need computing capacity without having to invest heavily in their own servers.

The decision to launch AWS, which was initially viewed as sceptical, proved that Bezos had the ability to recognise changing market needs and direct them to new innovations that would open up huge business opportunities. Today, AWS is one of the main pillars of Amazon's revenue and allows the company to maintain its position as one of the biggest players in the technology industry.

Bezos also adapted to changing consumption patterns. Amazon Prime, which was launched in 2005, changed the way people buy things online. By providing additional benefits such as free two-day shipping, Bezos entices customers to shop and subscribe to the service more often. This is a strategic move that demonstrates his ability to anticipate changing consumer needs and leverage it to strengthen Amazon's position in the market.

In addition, Bezos is very adaptive to the great challenges that come along the Amazon journey. For example, in 2015, Bezos and his team decided to invest heavily in the Amazon Echo and Alexa voice assistant. At the time, voice assistant technology wasn't popular enough, and some people doubted the potential of this product. However, he has a vision to create a device that allows people to interact with their technology in a more natural and human way. Today, Alexa is one of Amazon's best-selling products and strengthens the company's position in the home technology and smart device market.

Jeff Bezos teaches us that as leaders, it's not enough to just stick with what's already in place. Adaptive leadership involves being ready to change direction when the market moves in a new direction and to look for new opportunities in the midst of existing challenges. He has always demonstrated his ability to respond quickly to change and steer Amazon to sectors that are not only relevant at the time but also prepare the organisation for a greater future.

Bezos' leadership proves that adaptive and visionary leaders are able to see far beyond current market trends and anticipate what is to come. This adaptability is not just about responding to external changes but also about creating change itself, making him one of the most influential business leaders in the world.

Empathy

At the core of innovation leadership, there is the value of empathy that guides us on our journey to understand and connect with those we serve. Empathy is the ability to see the world through the eyes of others, feel what they are feeling, and understand their needs and desires deeply. It's about getting out of ourselves and walking in the shoes of others, not just to see their perspective but to really understand the feelings and motivations behind them. This trait is essential for leaders who want to create products, services, and experiences that truly touch the hearts of their audiences.

Empathy in innovation leadership is more than just customer satisfaction; it's about building a bond that speaks directly to the core of the user experience. It's about designing solutions that are not only functional but also emotional and significant. It requires a deep dive into the lives of those we want to serve, listening attentively, observing carefully, and interacting sincerely. Through empathy, leaders can identify unmet needs, neglected problems, and unexpressed desires, turning them into opportunities for innovation that can change lives for the better.

One of the most inspiring stories about empathy in action is Steve Jobs and the creation of the iPhone. Before the iPhone, mobile phones were generally utilitarian devices focussed on basic functions such as calling and sending text messages. They were tools without a deep emotional bond with their users. However, Jobs looked beyond just the functional aspects of the phone. He envisioned a device that was not just a tool but an integral part of people's lives—a device that not only met practical needs but could also inspire and excite people.

Jobs' empathic understanding of users' desire for simplicity, beauty, and functionality drove the development of the iPhone. He and his team embarked on a relentless search for a design that was not only intuitive but also elegant, removing the complexity that stood in the way of other smartphones. The iPhone had to be so easy to use that it could be operated with just the touch of a finger, in stark contrast to the devices of the time that relied on a stylus.

This empathetic approach pervades every aspect of the iPhone, from the minimalist design to the way the device responds to the user's touch with immediate and tangible feedback. Jobs' deep understanding of users' desire for connected digital experiences led to the development of features such as the App Store, which transformed the iPhone from just a phone into a platform for endless possibilities.

The launch of the iPhone in 2007 was a major turning point in the world of technology. This is not only the launch of a new phone but also the beginning of a new era in the way people interact with technology. iPhone revolutionised the smartphone industry, setting new standards in design, functionality, and user experience. It shows how empathy can drive innovation, resulting in products that truly intersect with the user.

The story of Steve Jobs and the iPhone teaches us that behind great innovation, there is an ability to empathise—to truly understand the needs, wants, and challenges of those we try to serve. This shows that when leaders listen with empathy, they can create solutions that not only meet the practical needs of users but also touch their lives in meaningful ways.

Empathy, therefore, is not only a characteristic of innovation leadership; it is a fundamental principle that fuels the creative process. It encourages leaders to look beyond what it seems, to explore the depths of the human experience, and to design solutions that are not only innovative but also truly human. In a world that is constantly evolving with technological advancements, empathy remains a reminder that the best innovations are the ones that can connect with us on a personal level, making our lives better, easier, and more fulfilling.

Empower the Team

At the heart of innovation leadership, there is a value that is often taken for granted but is critical: Empowering Teams. Strong leadership lies not only in the ability to make big decisions and set direction but also in the ability to empower those around us to take initiative, grow, and innovate. Empowering a team means providing trust, providing space for experimentation, and creating an environment where each individual feels valued, empowered, and motivated to give their best. Leadership is not about being the centre of attention but about creating a team that is able to stand alone, grow, and create exceptional solutions.

Empowering teams doesn't mean giving up control entirely but rather giving them space to make their own decisions, overcome challenges, and innovate their ways. It involves removing barriers that stand in the way of creativity, providing access to needed resources, and recognising each contribution with respect and appreciation. When a leader empowers his team, they give the team the confidence to take responsibility, which in turn encourages a sense of ownership and better performance.

One outstanding example of empowering a team comes from Pixar Animation Studios, under the leadership of Ed Catmull and John Lasseter. Since its inception, Pixar has been a place where creativity and technology meet to create magic. However, they did not achieve such success simply because of strong leadership; they empowered each team member to contribute to the maximum. Pixar movie ideas don't just arise from directions or assumptions from superiors but can be born from anyone on the team. Every individual, whether an animator, writer, or technician, is given the freedom to innovate, come up with new ideas and collaborate to solve creative problems.

For example, when Pixar worked on the movie *Toy Story*, they adopted a strong collaborative culture, which gave the team members the freedom to contribute with their ideas. In story and character development, ideas are not limited to just the director or studio leader. Instead, the freedom to explore new ideas from different departments—without the pressure to follow the vision of the boss alone—encourages great creativity. Every team member feels like they have a voice, and it fosters a great sense of confidence, passion, and creativity throughout the company.

Leadership that empowers teams is not just about overcoming challenges together but also about celebrating successes together. When *Toy Story* was finally launched in 1995 and became a huge success, it was not only a victory for Pixar's leaders but a victory for the entire team that had been empowered to take on a role in the journey. Everyone involved feels like they have a part in that success, and this is one of the reasons why Pixar continues to create amazing, innovative films.

The story of Pixar shows how important it is to empower teams in innovation. Empowering leadership is not just about giving orders or achieving goals but about creating a culture that fosters confidence, freedom to experiment, and opportunities to grow. When teams feel empowered, they not only work to achieve the leader's vision, but they also co-create that vision.

Empowering leadership means giving teams the opportunity to take risks, innovate, and find new ways to solve problems. This means giving them trust, support, and resources to bring their ideas to life. It's not about control but about creating an environment that allows creativity to thrive and every team member feels valued.

By empowering a team, a leader not only creates innovative solutions but also builds a team that has a stronger commitment to shared success. Empowering leadership will always be more than just making the right decisions—it's what creates continuous innovation and unstoppable strength in the face of challenges.

Chapter 4: Building a Culture of Innovation

Creating a Safe Space for Innovation

In the great journey to build a culture of innovation in an organisation, the foundation on which creativity and breakthrough are based is to create a safe space for innovation. This basic principle goes beyond allocating resources or setting innovation quotas; it touches the core of an organisation, forming a sanctuary where ideas, both big and small, can grow and develop without fear.

A safe space for innovation is an environment that accepts the uncertainty of the creative process. It acknowledged that the path to breakthrough ideas is often fraught with failures, wrong steps, and difficult lessons. In this space, individuals feel empowered to express their opinions, experiment with new concepts, and challenge the status quo, with the belief that their efforts are valued, not just seen in the end result. This atmosphere of psychological safety is very important because this is where the seeds of innovation are sown by mutual trust, openness, and a collective commitment to explore and discover.

Creating a safe space for innovation requires leaders who are not just administrators but 'gardeners' of human potential. They take care of their organisation with gentle hands, ensuring that each individual gets sunlight in the form of encouragement, water in the form of resources, and soil in the form of support necessary to grow. These leaders understand that innovation is not a decision that comes down from the top but rather an emergence from the bottom, where breakthrough ideas often come from the bottom, from those closest to the job, the customer, and the challenge at hand.

Google's Aristotle Project is a very clear example of how creating a safe space for innovation can unleash unprecedented levels of creativity and collaboration. The project was launched to uncover effective team codes and found that the highest-performing teams were those whose members felt psychologically safe. These teams allow people to take risks without feeling insecure or embarrassed, where every voice is heard and where the human element of teamwork is valued above all else.

Inspired by these findings, Google embarked on a mission to foster this kind of environment across its organisation. They support the principles of psychological safety, encourage employees to take risks, express their opinions, and learn from failure without fear of retaliation. This approach turns Google into a bastion of innovation, a place where new ideas abound and are celebrated, from the development of revolutionary products like Google Search and Gmail to pioneering ventures in artificial intelligence and quantum computing.

Creating a safe space for innovation, as Google points out, is not about big spending or massive gestures; it's about building an environment where every individual feels seen, heard, and valued. It's about building a culture where the question of "What if?" is greeted with encouragement, not scepticism, where the quest for the unknown is a collective adventure, not a personal gamble.

At its core, a safe space for innovation is the foundation that organisations can build to create a future that is not only imagined but actively pursued. This is where the carpet of the future is woven from the threads of dreams, ideas, and the courage to step into the unknown. Creating a space like this is a testament to an organisation's commitment to not only achieving greatness but doing so in a way that uplifts, empowers, and inspires every individual along the way.

So, the journey towards innovation begins not with the first step but with the planting of a garden where every seed of an idea has the opportunity to become something extraordinary. It is a testament to the power of psychological security, the magic of collective belief, and the limitless potential that exists in an environment that dares to say, "Here, you are safe to dream, to try, to fail, and to fly."

Encouraging Risk-Taking and Experimentation

In the grand narrative of building a culture of innovation, the chapter on encouraging risk-taking and experimentation is a testament to the spirit of exploration and the courage to discover new things. It's not just about the courage to take risks but about embracing failure as a stepping stone to greatness. This ethos is not just about tolerating risk; it's about pushing it and understanding that the path to great innovation is filled with trials, errors, and valuable lessons that can only be learned through a challenging journey.

Encouraging risk-taking and experimentation is like sailing into an uncharted ocean, not carelessly but with a firm heart, guided by the stars of curiosity and the compass of creativity. It is a journey that requires courage and resilience, where the quest for innovation is driven by a shared belief in the potential of "what can happen." In this culture, failure is not a sign of disgrace but a symbol of honour, proof that someone dared to push the boundaries of what's possible.

Leaders in this culture are not just supervisors; they are exploration captains, inspiring their teams with a vision of a new land rich in innovation. They understood that in order to discover new territory, one had to dare to leave the safe shores. Thus, they create an environment where experimentation is celebrated, where every attempt—successful or unsuccessful—is a valuable lesson in the progress roadmap.

A vivid example of this principle can be found in the story of 3M, a conglomerate known for its innovation and the birthplace of Post-it Note. The product, which is now a staple on desks around the world, is not the result of a deliberate effort to create sticky notes. Rather, it is an unexpected result of an experiment that is considered a 'failure.' Spencer Silver, a scientist at 3M, is trying to develop a super-strong adhesive. Instead, he created a weak adhesive that could be reused. For years, this 'failure' seemed useless until his colleague, Art Fry, frustrated by his frequently falling bookmarks, saw the new potential of Silver's invention. The rest is history. 3M's Post-it Note is more than just a product; it is a symbol of what can be achieved when an organisation fully embraces risk-taking and experimentation. It shows how a culture that encourages curiosity and freedom to explore can lead to unexpected discoveries. 3M supports this culture with a '15% Time' policy, where employees can spend some of their working time on projects they are interested in, even if those projects are not part of their official duties. This policy recognises that innovation cannot be scheduled or forced; innovation should be given room to grow naturally from the seeds of curiosity and experimentation.

Encouraging risk-taking and experimentation means understanding that the path to innovation is not straight. It's a winding path filled with unexpected turns, dead ends, and shortcuts. It's about realising that the greatest innovations often arise from the courage to venture into unfamiliar territory, armed with questions and the courage to seek answers.

In building a culture where risk-taking and experimentation are celebrated, organisations like 3M create fertile ground for innovation to thrive. They understood that every failed experiment was one step closer to discovery, and every risk taken was a leap into the future. This approach not only results in innovative products and services but also shapes an ever-growing ecosystem of learning and growth.

As such, the chapter on encouraging risk-taking and experimentation is a reminder that at the heart of every innovative culture lies the spirit of adventure. It is a call for organisations and leaders to strengthen their teams, ignite the flames of curiosity and courage, and together embark on a noble journey to innovation. On this journey, every failure is a story of resilience, every risk is a testament to courage, and every experiment is a step towards a star of discovery.

Presenting Awards and Recognition for Innovation

Have you ever thought that mere appreciation can be the fuel that ignites the spirit of innovation? Recognising and rewarding innovation is not just about giving away trophies; this is the organisation's way of saying, "We see your courage to try something different." This is not just an annual appreciation ritual but an ongoing recognition that encourages everyone to think boldly and push boundaries.

Appreciating innovation is about building a culture that loves the creative process, one that not only assesses results but also has the courage to take the first step. Imagine an environment where every idea counts as valuable—where employees feel valued for their initiatives and experiments, even when the results aren't perfect. This is where innovation can flourish without limits, where every mistake is a step towards greater success.

For example, Adobe has proven the power of awards and recognition in innovation. With programs like 'Kickbox'—a red box given to each employee that contains experimental funds, resources for idea development, and innovation guidance—Adobe empowers every individual to research, test, and create something new. They are not only given permission but invited to experiment and innovate without fear of failure. This red box has generated various ideas that have gone on to become successful products and services, including new features in Adobe Creative Suite.

The Kickbox program begins by providing employees with a red box containing $1,000 in funds to start their project. In addition to funds, the box is also equipped with tools and guides in the form of books that provide practical steps to develop ideas. This creates space for each individual to test their own hypotheses, develop ideas that may not seem potential at first, and encourage them to think creatively without fear of failure. So, every employee can feel that they have full responsibility for the success or failure of their idea.

However, what sets Kickbox apart is not just the provision of funds or resources but how Adobe accommodates failed ideas in a constructive way. Employees are encouraged to fail as quickly as possible, learn from mistakes, and continue their experiments without shame. It removes the stigma of failure that often haunts many people in the corporate world, thus creating a culture focussed on continuous innovation. In this way, the program makes failure a very important part of the process and not an obstacle that needs to be avoided.

What's more interesting is that successful projects are not only rewarded but also given the opportunity to scale or implement at the enterprise level. For example, many of the new features in Adobe Creative Cloud were born from ideas that started with Kickbox. This shows that when awards and recognition are not only in the form of praise but also supported by real opportunities to develop and implement ideas, innovation becomes more measurable and has a big impact.

This Kickbox giveaway from Adobe is more than just a tool; it is a symbol of the company's trust and confidence in the potential of its employees. Result? Big ideas are emerging, not from top management, but from the hands of innovators at all levels. *Aha!* This is what happens when innovation is not only measured by the success of the product but by the courage to try and keep trying.

So, if we're talking about creating an innovative culture, don't just focus on the end result. Focus on the people, on their journey. Because, the greatest innovation often comes from people who feel cared for, appreciated, and supported. This is the 'aha moment' that inspires us all: that by appreciating every small step, we are actually building a foothold for the next big leap.

Aligning Innovation with Organisational Goals

Have you ever wondered how industry-changing companies can survive and thrive? The key is to align innovation with organisational goals. Without a clear direction, innovation will only become a futile experiment. To achieve maximum results, innovation must move in tandem with the larger organisational goals. This is what Wise, a fintech company that has overhauled the way the world views international remittances, is doing.

Wise (formerly TransferWise) understands that to become a leader in the global financial industry, they can't just create a new product or feature without a clear goal. Their mission is to reduce costs and non-transparency in international remittances, as well as give users greater control over their money. Their innovations are always moving in tandem with this goal, ensuring that every step they take strengthens their great mission.

Aligning innovation with organisational goals for Wise is all about providing relevant and transparent solutions to the problems their users face. One real-world example is the Wise Borderless Account, which allows users to store money in multiple currencies, accept international payments, and manage their expenses in a much more efficient and transparent way compared to traditional bank accounts. Not only does this feature offer convenience, but it is also in line with Wise's goal of giving users full control over their finances without any hidden fees or confusing systems.

In addition, Wise developed Wise Business, a service for entrepreneurs and small businesses who want to send money internationally without the high fees that traditional banks charge. This service supports their goal of making international transactions easier, faster, and more affordable. By eliminating excessive fees, Wise opens up access to international markets for many small businesses that were previously constrained by high transaction fees.

Wise's innovations are not only focussed on technology but rather on a deep understanding of the needs of their users. By aligning each innovation with the goal of providing a cheaper, faster, and more transparent service, the company has not only managed to solve the problem of international money transfers but also built trust and loyalty among its users.

Wise shows that aligning innovation with organisational goals not only supports growth but also creates a broader positive impact. By focusing on a clear goal, it is able to create solutions that are truly relevant to market needs and change the way people perceive and transact internationally. Innovation that aligns with organisational goals gives companies the power to survive and thrive while delivering real value to their users.

In conclusion, innovation that is directed and aligned with the organisation's goals creates a solid foundation for sustainable growth and change. Through Wise's example, we can see how a clear mission-guided innovation can bring about significant change, not only for companies but also for the global community. Innovation is not only about technology but about providing solutions that are meaningful, relevant, and truly overcome existing challenges.

Chapter 5: Innovation Strategy: Ensuring Successful Innovation

What Is Innovation Strategy?

An innovation strategy in business refers to a shared commitment to a common innovation objective and a structured set of activities intended to support the future growth and development of an organisation. It encompasses an organisation's focus on different types of innovations, such as product, process, or business model, and the corresponding allocation of resources to achieve its strategic goals at the corporate and business unit levels.

The Importance of Innovation Strategy

Innovation is crucial for businesses to achieve and sustain a competitive advantage in the marketplace. Successful innovation allows organisations to create value by developing new products, services, or processes that meet evolving customer needs or preferences. As noted by Schumpeter, innovation is particularly important for organisations to survive and thrive during major economic downturns. Indeed, research has shown that innovation can serve as a catalyst for business growth and success. Innovative companies are better equipped to adapt to changes in their environment and deliver superior products or services that give them a competitive edge.

Innovation strategy is not merely a choice but a necessity for long-term sustainability in the fast-paced world of business. In an era marked by rapid technological advancements and shifting customer expectations, companies that fail to innovate risk falling behind their competitors. Innovation enables them to not only address current market demands but also anticipate future trends, positioning themselves as forward-thinking leaders in their industries. By integrating a proactive innovation strategy, businesses can better manage uncertainty and respond with agility to unforeseen market shifts, enhancing their resilience in the face of adversity.

Furthermore, an effective innovation strategy allows organisations to optimise internal processes, improve operational efficiency, and reduce costs. For example, many companies have adopted digital transformation initiatives, incorporating technologies such as artificial intelligence and automation to streamline workflows and boost productivity. Such innovations do not just lead to cost savings; they also improve the quality and speed of service delivery, ultimately enhancing customer satisfaction. By prioritising innovation in processes as well as products, businesses create a foundation for sustainable growth that adapts over time.

Companies that strategically invest in innovation also foster a culture of creativity and continuous improvement among their workforce. Employees are encouraged to think outside the box, experiment with new ideas, and contribute to a culture that values innovation. This, in turn, increases engagement and motivation as employees feel more empowered and integral to the company's success. Firms that prioritise innovation often become desirable employers, attracting top talent that brings diverse perspectives and skills necessary for driving further advancements.

In conclusion, an innovation strategy is indispensable for businesses aiming to stay competitive and relevant. Beyond creating value and boosting profits, it builds resilience, encourages efficiency, and cultivates a culture of continuous learning and adaptability. When businesses commit to strategic innovation, they position themselves not only to survive in fluctuating market conditions but to lead and shape the future of their industries.

Key Components of a Successful Innovation Strategy

- Establish a compelling vision and mission
- Obtaining buy-in from the CEO and key stakeholders
- Strong leadership
- Strategic business thinking
- Identify and analyse innovation opportunities
- Allocate resources effectively to support innovation efforts
- Cultivate a culture of innovation and risk-taking
- A strategically balanced innovation portfolio

- A concrete, executable innovation blueprint
- Measure and evaluate innovation performance

Establish a Compelling Vision and Mission

The foundation of any successful innovation strategy is a clear and compelling vision and mission. The vision should reflect the company's purpose and long-term objectives, inspiring employees, stakeholders, and customers alike. A well-defined mission also provides a sense of direction for innovation efforts, helping to align projects with the company's overall strategic goals. This alignment not only motivates teams but also ensures that every innovative initiative contributes to the broader business vision, enhancing coherence and commitment throughout the organisation.

To establish a truly compelling vision and mission, leaders must go beyond traditional statements and create narratives that resonate on an emotional level. This means crafting a vision that speaks not only to the organisation's ambitions but also to the aspirations of employees and stakeholders. When people see themselves as an integral part of a larger purpose, they feel more connected and empowered to innovate. The vision should be a driving force that excites and unites the organisation, building a shared understanding of the impact they are collectively working towards.

In addition, a mission that emphasises adaptability and forward-thinking is critical in today's rapidly changing market landscape. By defining innovation as a core part of the mission, companies signal their commitment to progress and responsiveness to new opportunities. This encourages teams to embrace a proactive mindset, consistently looking for ways to push boundaries and add value. When the mission embeds innovation at its core, it creates a culture where employees are more inclined to experiment and take calculated risks, knowing their efforts contribute to a future that aligns with the company's evolving goals.

Obtaining Buy-In from the CEO and Key Stakeholders

Obtaining buy-in from the CEO and key stakeholders is critical for the success of even the most robust innovation strategy. All those involved in its implementation, from the executive team to frontline employees, must comprehend and embrace the strategy. If all parties share a common understanding of the innovation vision and objectives, they can work cohesively towards the desired outcome without debating the directions. Securing this alignment and commitment across the organisation is crucial for translating innovation strategy into tangible results.

Gaining buy-in from the CEO and key stakeholders goes beyond just initial alignment; it requires sustained advocacy and visible support from leadership. When the CEO champions innovation openly, it sends a powerful message across the organisation, reinforcing that innovation is a priority and worthy of resource allocation. Key stakeholders need to see clear value in the strategy, not only for business growth but also for competitive positioning and long-term relevance. Regular updates, transparent reporting, and success stories can maintain their interest and confidence, ensuring that innovation remains an ongoing focus.

Moreover, engaging stakeholders early in the innovation process can foster a sense of ownership and accountability. By involving leaders in discussions around potential challenges, opportunities, and resource requirements, they become active contributors rather than passive supporters. This collaborative approach helps address concerns early on and enables the innovation team to gain valuable insights from experienced decision-makers. Ultimately, when stakeholders feel their input is valued and see the impact of their commitment, they're more likely to support the innovation journey through potential setbacks, sustaining momentum and paving the way for a culture of continuous improvement.

Strong Leadership

Effective innovation strategies also require strong leadership and the ability to institute organisational changes. Leaders play a critical role in developing and communicating a vision for innovation, as well as in creating the conditions for it to thrive. Leadership is indeed crucial for the success of any innovation strategy. Leaders set the tone for innovation by developing and clearly communicating a compelling vision that inspires and aligns teams with the organisation's goals. Their commitment to innovation becomes a guiding force, instilling confidence in employees and stakeholders. By articulating a vision that underscores the importance of creativity, experimentation, and resilience, leaders create a shared understanding of why innovation matters. This alignment helps teams see their contributions as essential to the organisation's long-term growth and success, fueling a sense of purpose and motivation that drives sustained innovation efforts.

Moreover, effective leaders foster an environment where innovation can flourish by actively shaping a culture that embraces change, risk-taking, and continuous learning. They encourage team members to think beyond traditional boundaries and support them in exploring new ideas, even if those ideas initially seem unconventional. Leaders who are willing to invest in the necessary resources, provide autonomy, and demonstrate openness to failure as part of the learning process to empower teams to take calculated risks. This supportive culture is essential for sparking creativity and enabling employees to experiment with new approaches, knowing they have the trust and backing of the management.

Finally, leaders play a pivotal role in instituting the organisational changes required to sustain innovation. Innovation strategies often necessitate shifts in structure, processes, or priorities to accommodate new projects and agile methods. Strong leaders can navigate these changes by fostering cross-functional collaboration, breaking down silos, and streamlining decision-making to enhance responsiveness. Their ability to drive organisational change helps integrate innovation into the company's DNA, ensuring it remains an ongoing, dynamic process rather than a one-time initiative. By leading with vision, creating an innovation-friendly culture, and steering necessary changes, leaders lay the foundation for a robust and adaptive innovation strategy.

Strategic Business Thinking

The development of a comprehensive innovation strategy involves several key components beyond just visionary leadership. A strategic business mindset is essential, as innovation must be firmly grounded in an understanding of the organisation's core competencies, market dynamics, and long-term competitive positioning. This strategic thinking helps identify the specific innovation opportunities that best align with the company's strengths and growth goals.

A strategically-minded approach to innovation begins with a thorough analysis of the organisation's internal capabilities, resources, and potential areas for improvement or expansion. This assessment allows leaders to pinpoint the most promising domains for innovation, where the company's expertise can be leveraged to create unique value. The strategic innovation process also requires a deep understanding of the external landscape, including market trends, customer needs, and competitor activities. By synthesising internal and external insights, organisations can develop a clear innovation strategy that responds to unmet market demands while building upon their own competitive advantages.

This strategic focus extends to the prioritisation and sequencing of innovation initiatives. Rather than pursuing innovation haphazardly, a strategic approach involves carefully selecting and timing the most impactful projects based on their alignment with the organisation's goals, resource constraints, and market readiness. Strategically-minded leaders understand that innovation is not an end in itself but a means to an end—a vehicle for achieving sustainable competitive advantage and long-term business success.

Identifying and Analysing Innovation Opportunities

Identifying and analysing innovation opportunities is a distinct yet interconnected process that builds upon strategic business thinking. While strategic thinking focuses on aligning innovation with long-term business goals, identifying opportunities is about recognising and exploring specific areas where innovation can drive change. This process often involves conducting market research, monitoring industry trends, and engaging with customers to uncover unmet needs or pain points that could be addressed through new products, services, or processes.

To identify innovation opportunities, companies need to stay attuned to shifts in customer demands, emerging technologies, and market gaps. By analysing competitive actions, customer feedback, and technological advancements, businesses can uncover areas ripe for innovation. However, simply recognising potential opportunities isn't enough—leaders must then assess their feasibility and alignment with strategic goals. This ensures that identified opportunities are not only relevant to market needs but also fit within the company's capabilities and resources. By blending this opportunity identification with strategic thinking, companies can prioritise initiatives that are not only innovative but also strategically significant, increasing the likelihood of long-term success.

Allocate Resources Effectively to Support Innovation Efforts

Once innovation opportunities are identified, the next critical step is to allocate resources effectively. Innovation requires investment in terms of time, money, and talent. Companies must allocate resources strategically to ensure innovation efforts have the support needed for success. This involves not only funding innovative projects but also dedicating skilled personnel and the right technologies to bring ideas to life. Resource allocation should also be agile, allowing for quick adjustments based on project progress or shifts in the market landscape, ensuring that innovation initiatives stay relevant and effective.

Effective resource allocation also involves balancing short-term priorities with long-term innovation goals. While it's important to allocate resources to immediate needs, a successful innovation strategy requires a forward-thinking approach that invests in future growth. Companies should consider funding initiatives that might not show immediate returns but have the potential for significant long-term impact. This means having a portfolio approach to resource allocation, where some resources are dedicated to incremental innovations that deliver quick wins, while others are invested in more disruptive or transformative projects that may take longer to materialise but offer greater rewards.

Additionally, fostering a culture of innovation requires allocating time and space for employees to explore creative solutions without the pressure of immediate results. This can include providing employees with dedicated 'innovation time,' similar to Google's 20% time, where they can work on projects outside their regular duties. By creating an environment where experimentation is encouraged and supported, businesses can increase their chances of uncovering breakthrough innovations. Investing in professional development, training, and cross-functional collaboration also strengthens the overall innovation ecosystem by ensuring that teams have the skills and knowledge needed to execute innovative ideas successfully.

Cultivate a Culture of Innovation and Risk-Taking

A culture that encourages experimentation, risk-taking, and learning from failures is essential for innovation. Employees should feel safe to propose new ideas and test uncharted approaches without fear of repercussions for failure. Organisations can foster this culture by recognising and rewarding creativity, encouraging collaboration, and providing platforms for employees to share insights. Leaders play a critical role here, modelling innovative behaviour and demonstrating a commitment to innovation as a core company value.

To cultivate a culture of innovation and risk-taking, it's essential to establish an environment where learning from failure is not seen as a setback but as a stepping stone to growth. Leaders must actively support their teams by reframing failure as an opportunity to pivot, adapt, and improve. This mindset shift is crucial for breaking the cycle of fear that often stifles creativity and new ideas. Encouraging risk-taking also means empowering employees with the tools and resources they need to experiment confidently, whether that be time, funding, or access to mentors and experts within the organisation.

Additionally, organisations should create structures that facilitate the free flow of ideas. Cross-functional teams, innovation hubs, or dedicated 'idea incubators' can serve as fertile grounds for creative collaboration. When diverse minds come together, they can challenge each other's assumptions, generate new solutions, and push boundaries in ways that a single department or siloed team might struggle to do. Recognising and celebrating those who dare to take risks—regardless of the outcome—signals to the entire organisation that innovation is valued above all. When risk is embraced, it's not about reckless abandonment but about calculated experimentation that paves the way for the future.

A Strategically-Balanced Innovation Portfolio

Successful innovation strategies involve a portfolio approach, designating appropriate funding and talent for various types of innovation efforts, from incremental improvements to disruptive breakthroughs. Furthermore, companies should ensure that their innovation efforts are supported by the appropriate organisational structure, processes, and incentives.

A strategically balanced innovation portfolio guarantees that organisations are not solely focussed on one type of innovation at the expense of others. Firms should divide their resources across different innovation categories—incremental, adjacent, and disruptive. Incremental innovations, such as small product improvements or operational efficiencies, provide a steady stream of value and help maintain competitive advantage. Meanwhile, adjacent innovations explore new markets or slightly altered products, tapping into new growth opportunities without taking on the same level of risk as disruptive innovations. Finally, disruptive innovations, while risky, can lead to radical transformation and market leadership if executed successfully. A well-rounded portfolio mitigates risk by ensuring that the organisation is not overly dependent on any single approach.

To maximise the effectiveness of this portfolio, it's crucial for organisations to establish the right support structures. This includes defining clear processes for how different types of innovation are managed, from ideation through to execution and scaling. Incentives should align with long-term goals, encouraging teams to take the right amount of risk and invest in the most promising opportunities. Moreover, companies must ensure that the organisational culture and leadership are adaptive to changing market conditions, so that they can pivot or scale innovations accordingly. By balancing short-term gains with long-term visionary projects, organisations can sustain continuous growth while positioning themselves for breakthrough innovations when the time is right.

A Concrete, Executable Innovation Blueprint

A concrete, executable innovation blueprint serves as the roadmap that bridges the gap between ambitious ideas and tangible results. It begins with a clear vision and setting specific, measurable goals that align with the company's strategic objectives. This vision should not only define what the innovation aims to achieve but also outline the steps and resources required for its success. Key milestones should be established to track progress, ensuring that the team stays on course and adapts to any unforeseen challenges. An effective blueprint also incorporates a flexible framework that allows for course correction, recognising that the path to innovation is rarely linear.

The blueprint must detail the structure and responsibilities needed to execute the plan. Assigning roles to individuals and teams with the right expertise ensures that there's ownership at every stage of the innovation process. Clear lines of communication are crucial, enabling collaboration across departments and ensuring that all stakeholders are aligned. Additionally, the blueprint should specify the tools, technologies, and methodologies to be used, including timelines for testing, scaling, and feedback loops. By breaking down the process into manageable phases, the team can remain agile while focusing on delivering outcomes rather than just pursuing lofty ideas.

Equally important is the process of identifying potential risks and challenges that may arise throughout the innovation journey. A concrete blueprint should include a risk management strategy, anticipating obstacles such as resource constraints, technological limitations, or market resistance. By proactively addressing these risks, the team can develop contingency plans to minimise disruptions and maintain momentum. The blueprint should also incorporate strategies for managing change within the organisation, ensuring that innovation efforts are supported and embraced across all levels. This foresight helps build resilience into the execution plan, allowing the organisation to adapt quickly and efficiently when faced with unexpected hurdles.

Measure and Evaluate Innovation Performance

Measuring and evaluating innovation performance is critical for understanding whether innovation efforts are yielding the desired outcomes and contributing to long-term success. It starts with defining clear and relevant metrics that align with the organisation's strategic goals. These metrics can include factors such as the number of new products launched, revenue generated from innovations, market share growth, and customer satisfaction improvements. By establishing both qualitative and quantitative indicators, companies can get a comprehensive view of their innovation performance. For instance, customer feedback and market adoption rates provide insights into the value of innovations from the consumer's perspective, while financial metrics can show how these innovations translate into revenue or cost savings.

Evaluating innovation performance also involves assessing the efficiency of the innovation process itself. This includes measuring how quickly ideas are brought to market, the cost-effectiveness of innovation activities, and the return on investment (ROI) for innovation projects. Organisations should track the time taken from ideation to execution, as well as the resources consumed in the process. By identifying bottlenecks or inefficiencies, companies can optimise their workflows and processes to accelerate innovation cycles. Furthermore, an ongoing evaluation of resource allocation ensures that the most promising projects are prioritised, while less effective initiatives are either refined or phased out.

Beyond the direct outputs of innovation, it's essential to assess the broader impact of innovation efforts on the company culture and competitive position. Successful innovation should foster a culture of continuous improvement, collaboration, and risk-taking.

Evaluating how innovation initiatives influence employee engagement, talent retention, and organisational adaptability is just as important as measuring financial results. Additionally, tracking how innovation helps the company stay ahead of competitors and adapt to changing market conditions ensures that the organisation remains resilient and forward-thinking. By regularly measuring and evaluating innovation performance, companies can ensure their innovation strategies are dynamic, effective, and aligned with their overall vision for growth.

Example of Success Stories of Innovation Strategy

Let's begin with the example of Lego.

Lego, a renowned toy company, is a prime example of a successful innovation strategy. The company has a long history of innovation and adapting to changing market trends and customer preferences. Its innovation strategy has centred on a combination of incremental and radical innovations, allowing the company to maintain its core product offerings while also introducing new and exciting products that captivate its target audience.

One key aspect of Lego's innovation strategy has been its focus on understanding and anticipating customer needs. The company invests heavily in market research and customer feedback, using this information to guide its product development and innovation efforts. This deep understanding of its customers has enabled Lego to create products that resonate with its target market and consistently deliver value.

Moreover, Lego has also demonstrated a strong commitment to allocating resources effectively to support its innovation efforts. The company has a dedicated team of designers, engineers, and researchers who work collaboratively to identify new opportunities and bring innovative ideas to life. Lego also invests in state-of-the-art technology and production facilities to ensure the company can quickly and efficiently bring its innovations to market.

In addition to its focus on customer needs and resource allocation, Lego has also cultivated a culture that encourages and supports innovation. It has a strong leadership team that is committed to fostering a creative and collaborative environment where employees are empowered to take risks and explore new ideas.

Another example of a successful innovation strategy is that of Pixar, the renowned animation studio. Pixar's innovation strategy has been centred on the development of a strong creative culture that fosters innovation and collaboration across the organisation.

One key aspect of Pixar's innovation strategy is its emphasis on the involvement of all employees in the innovation process. The company has a flat organisational structure that encourages open communication and collaboration, allowing employees at all levels to contribute to the creative process.

Pixar has also demonstrated a strong commitment to

supporting the emergence of new ideas through both top-down and bottom-up approaches. The company's leadership team actively encourages and supports the development of new ideas, while also providing employees with the resources, autonomy, and opportunities they need to explore their own innovative concepts. Pixar fosters a culture that values creativity, collaboration, and risk-taking, empowering its workforce to contribute to the innovation process at all levels of the organisation.

Another critical component of Pixar's innovation strategy is its ability to accept and learn from failure. The company recognises that failure is an inevitable part of the innovation process and has developed a culture that embraces it as an opportunity for growth and learning.

Innovation Strategy Framework

The innovation process strategy from planning to implementation

- Planning: At the heart of a successful innovation strategy lies the planning phase, where organisations establish a clear vision and direction for their innovation efforts. During this stage, companies define their innovation goals, identify focus areas, and allocate resources accordingly.
- Discovery and Exploration: Successful innovation strategies encourage a continuous process of discovery and exploration, where organisations actively seek out new ideas, technologies, and market opportunities. This

involves a mix of top-down and bottom-up approaches, allowing leadership to set strategic direction while also empowering employees at all levels to contribute their own ideas and insights.

- Ideation: The ideation phase involves generating, evaluating, and selecting the most promising ideas that align with the organisation's strategic objectives. Engaging employees, customers, and external partners in the ideation process can lead to a diverse range of innovative solutions. Once the most promising ideas have been selected, the organisation can begin the process of development and prototyping.

- Evaluation and Selection: After the ideation stage, organisations must carefully evaluate and select the ideas that have the greatest potential for success. Criteria for evaluation may include market potential, alignment with strategic goals, technical feasibility, and financial viability.

- Implementation: Transforming ideas into tangible products, services, or processes requires a robust implementation plan. This phase involves securing internal buy-in, allocating necessary resources, and carefully managing the development and launch of new initiatives.

- Measurement: Monitoring and measuring the outcomes of innovation efforts is crucial for understanding their impact and informing future strategies. Establishing relevant metrics and tracking key performance indicators can help organisations evaluate the success of their innovation initiatives.

Corporate Innovation Strategy Framework

Source: adjusted from innovatestrategy.com

Decide the Focus Area of Innovation

The framework categorises corporate innovation initiatives based on their focus area and type of innovation. This results in four distinct quadrants: optimise, improve, create, and reinvent. A follow-up blog post examines the appropriate team structures, budgeting approaches, and return on investment considerations for each of these quadrants.

When positioned in the **optimise quadrant**, the goal is to enhance the organisation's operations. This involves streamlining processes and improving value creation. A small, focussed team typically performs best in this context, as success criteria can be easily determined by referencing the current state as a baseline. To optimise existing value-creation processes, individuals with deep process expertise, experienced facilitators, and method experts who can manage team dynamics and foster a productive work environment are required. From a budgetary perspective, these teams primarily incur time-related costs, and they should be able to generate efficiency gains that exceed their cumulative expenses.

In the **improve quadrant,** the focus is on enhancing the customer experience and refining existing products and services. The 'two-pizza rule' is often applicable in this context as well. Conducting customer interviews and analysing qualitative data is an activity that most organisations do not regularly engage in. If the necessary skills are not available in-house, it may be beneficial to bring in expert support. The Return on Investment can be relatively straightforward to measure, such as through an increased customer acquisition rate due to an improved sign-up process. However, the ROI can also manifest in less directly observable behaviours, such as a reduction in customers switching to competitors' products. Investing in a seamless customer experience generally yields favourable returns. Additionally, there may be beneficial spillover effects, such as a decrease in the number of calls to the contact centre due to an intuitive user experience.

When positioned in the **create quadrant,** the focus should be on developing innovative products and new services that can drive future revenue growth. Achieving this requires assembling a team with unique mindsets and skillsets - individuals who can envision and conceptualise solutions that do not currently exist. Here, it may be prudent to deviate from the 'two-pizza rule,' as smaller teams of 3 to 5 members, not necessarily industry experts, tend to be more effective at creating future business opportunities. In this context, the emphasis should not be on immediate return on investment, as many of the future product or service ideas may not ultimately come to fruition. Rather, the organisation must be willing to invest in potential 'losers' in order to uncover the eventual 'winners.' Moreover, it may take years before a new product or service begins generating revenue. Effective methods in this quadrant include hacking industry conventions and cultural beliefs, as well as driving innovation through a shift in meaning.

The **reinvent quadrant** represents a transformative innovation strategy. Organisations operating in this space are tasked with reimagining their core business and developing groundbreaking business models that can disrupt entire industries. This requires assembling a team of unconventional thinkers who are willing to challenge conventional wisdom and rethink the status quo. It is crucial to avoid hiring individuals solely based on industry expertise, as they may be predisposed to a particular way of thinking. Instead, the focus should be on recruiting creative minds who can think outside the boundaries of what is considered normal. When pursuing reinvention, organisations must be prepared to make significant investments without the expectation of immediate returns. This endeavour should be approached as an experimental process, as success is not guaranteed. However, it is important to recognise that competitors may be undertaking similar efforts to disrupt the industry, making it essential for organisations to proactively reinvent themselves to maintain their competitive position.

Ten Types of Innovation Model

The *Ten Types of Innovation* framework developed by Doblin outlines ten distinct dimensions of innovation, which can be organised into three broad categories: configuration (focussed on the internal organisation), offering (focussed on the product or service), and experience (focussed on the customer experience).

Innovation is not only about creating new products and services, but also about finding new ways to create and deliver value to customers. Doblin's *Ten Types of Innovation* framework is a comprehensive model that categorises innovation into ten distinct types. This model provides organisations with a holistic view of how they can innovate in various aspects of their business to create more value. Let's dive into each of the ten types.

1. Business/Profit Model Innovation (Configuration)

Business model innovation is one of the most profound types of innovation because it redefines how an organisation creates, delivers, and captures value. This type of innovation focuses on altering the way a business operates and generates revenue. For example, companies like Netflix transformed the entertainment industry by moving from a DVD rental model to a subscription-based streaming service. Shifting the business model often requires significant changes in organisational structures, partnerships, and value propositions to meet the evolving needs of customers.

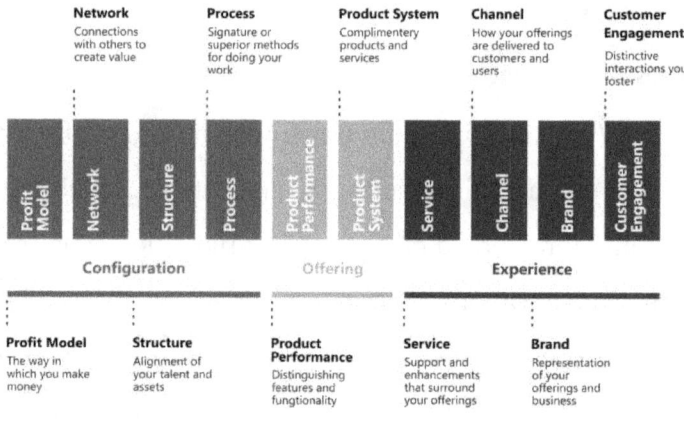

Source: doblin.com

2. Networking Innovation (Configuration)

Networking innovation focuses on creating new alliances, partnerships, and collaborations that allow a company to tap into new markets or leverage resources more effectively. It is about establishing connections with other organisations, individuals, or platforms that enhance the value offered to customers. Apple's collaboration with music companies to build the iTunes store is an example of networking innovation that revolutionised the music industry. By forming strategic networks, businesses can gain access to complementary expertise and resources that they wouldn't have been able to achieve independently.

3. Structure Innovation (Configuration)

Structure innovation refers to changes in the internal configuration of the organisation, such as how teams are organised, how workflows are managed, or how decision-making processes are structured. This type of innovation aims to optimise the company's internal operations to increase efficiency, reduce costs, or improve collaboration. Google's decision to allow employees to spend 20% of their time on passion projects, leading to innovations like Gmail and Google Maps, is an example of structure innovation that enhances creativity and productivity within an organisation.

4. Process Innovation (Configuration)

Process innovation focuses on improving the efficiency and effectiveness of an organisation's internal processes, such as production, delivery, and service provision. By optimising processes, organisations can reduce costs, speed up production, or improve the quality of their products or services. Toyota's implementation of lean manufacturing processes, which emphasised minimising waste and maximising efficiency, is a classic example of process innovation that transformed the automotive industry. This innovation not only improved profitability but also set new industry standards for quality and operational efficiency.

5. Product Performance Innovation (Offering)

Product performance innovation refers to improvements or enhancements made to the core attributes and features of a product or service. This could involve upgrading an existing product to make it more functional, durable, or powerful. It is typically what most people think of when they think about innovation—creating products that perform better or offer new capabilities. For instance, the continuous improvements to smartphones, such as better cameras, longer battery life, and faster processors, exemplify product performance innovation that meets growing consumer expectations and drives industry evolution.

6. Product System Innovation (Offering)

Product system innovation involves creating new combinations of products or services that work together as an integrated system. This could mean bundling products to provide a more comprehensive solution or integrating multiple functionalities into a single product. For example, Microsoft's Office Suite, which combines Word, Excel, PowerPoint, and other tools into one cohesive system, is an example of product system innovation. Such innovations not only improve the product's value proposition but also increase customer dependency on the integrated solution, enhancing user experience and driving customer loyalty.

7. Service Innovation (Offering)

Service innovation focuses on creating new or enhanced services that provide greater value to customers. This type of innovation is particularly important in industries such as hospitality, healthcare, and retail, where customer experience and service delivery are critical. For instance, companies like Uber have revolutionised the transportation industry by offering on-demand ride services via a mobile app, making transportation more convenient and accessible. Service innovation can significantly improve customer satisfaction by addressing pain points and providing new ways to interact with services.

8. Channel Innovation (Experience)

Channel innovation involves creating new ways to deliver products or services to customers or enhancing existing channels to improve access and engagement. This could include adopting new distribution channels, such as e-commerce, mobile apps, or direct-to-consumer models. For example, Amazon's development of its online marketplace was a groundbreaking channel innovation that reshaped how people buy products. By using digital platforms to offer a seamless shopping experience, companies can reach customers more effectively and provide greater convenience.

9. Brand Innovation (Experience)

Brand innovation is about creating a unique identity for a company or product that resonates with customers and differentiates it from competitors. This type of innovation focuses on shaping customer perceptions and building strong emotional connections with the brand. Companies like Nike, with its 'Just Do It' slogan and endorsement of athletes, have successfully innovated their brand to create a powerful, emotionally charged identity. Brand innovation plays a crucial role in how customers perceive value and align themselves with a brand's ethos, driving loyalty and advocacy.

10. Customer Engagement Innovation (Experience)

Customer engagement innovation revolves around enhancing the ways in which a company interacts with its customers throughout their journey. This involves creating meaningful and personalised experiences that deepen customer relationships and improve loyalty. For example, Starbucks has leveraged its loyalty program and mobile app to engage customers more effectively by offering personalised rewards, promotions, and services. This type of innovation focuses on building long-term relationships with customers through better communication, targeted offers, and interactive experiences that increase customer satisfaction and lifetime value.

Doblin's *Ten Types of Innovation* framework emphasises that organisations should not limit their innovation efforts to a single type or category. Instead, it's about creating a balanced approach that leverages innovation across various domains—whether in business models, processes, products, or customer experience—to maximise value and stay competitive in an ever-changing market. By exploring all ten types, companies can uncover new opportunities and develop a holistic strategy that drives sustainable growth and differentiation.

Chapter 6: Overcoming Challenges in Leading Innovation

Resistance to Change

Innovation is the lifeblood of progress, but guiding it forward is no simple feat. One of the towering obstacles in the path of innovation is the resistance to change. Understanding and overcoming this resistance is crucial for leaders and organisations seeking to innovate and stay ahead in a rapidly evolving world.

Resistance to change is a natural human inclination, stemming from the discomfort of leaving familiar grounds for the unknown. For many, the current state, despite its flaws, offers a comfort zone where predictability reigns. Venturing beyond this zone triggers fear, uncertainty, and a host of emotional defences, manifesting in various forms, from overt opposition to subtle procrastination. Tackling this resistance requires a blend of empathy, strategy, and perseverance.

Addressing resistance to change is not just a leadership challenge; it's a psychological journey that requires understanding why people hesitate to step away from familiar structures. Innovation demands embracing new systems and ideas, yet this journey often appears risky. Resistance can stem from a deep-seated sense of identity tied to existing processes and routines. When people perceive that changes threaten the very foundation of their professional identities or roles, the pushback can be intense. Leaders must recognise that for many, innovation signifies a personal upheaval, demanding a shift in both mindset and skills that feels intimidating.

Moreover, resistance can be reinforced by past experiences. Previous changes that didn't yield promised benefits or that were poorly implemented can create cynicism toward new initiatives. This 'change fatigue' is a real concern, where employees feel that innovation is a passing trend rather than a sustainable improvement. Addressing this requires not only clarifying the tangible benefits of the change but also involving people in the process, offering assurances, and creating a shared sense of ownership over new ideas. A culture of open communication and transparency helps in slowly dismantling the emotional walls that reinforce resistance.

Why Do People Resist Change?

People resist change for several reasons. Fear of the unknown is a prime factor, as individuals may worry about their ability to adapt to new processes, technologies, or roles. There's also the fear of failure, where the possibility of not meeting expectations in a new setting looms large. Loss of control is another concern, as changes often mean shifting power dynamics and altering routines, leading individuals to feel they are no longer in charge of their environment. Moreover, change can imply loss of status, comfort, or even employment. This perceived loss can trigger a defensive mechanism, causing individuals to cling to the status quo. Finally, a lack of trust in the leaders driving the change can exacerbate resistance.

Another layer to consider in understanding resistance is the role of social dynamics. People often resist change because of the influence of their peers and the cultural norms within their teams or organisations. When groups are tightly knit, there's a tendency to conform to established ways to avoid conflict or judgment. Social conformity can, therefore, become a barrier to change, as people may fear standing out or being perceived as too quick to adopt new ideas. This peer pressure can be subtle yet potent, creating an unspoken resistance to anything that disrupts the group's status quo.

Additionally, timing and communication around change play critical roles. If a change is perceived as sudden, employees may feel blindsided and resistance intensifies. People need time to mentally prepare and emotionally adjust to new expectations. Transparency from leaders about why changes are necessary, how they will unfold, and how each person fits into the new vision can alleviate feelings of unpredictability. Offering training and support during transitions reassures people that they won't be left to navigate unfamiliar processes alone, which can significantly reduce fear and build confidence in their ability to adapt.

Budget Allocation

Allocating a budget for innovation poses its own set of challenges, as it often requires diverting resources from other areas and justifying expenses that may not yield immediate returns. Innovation budgets are typically seen as high-risk, given the unpredictable outcomes associated with novel initiatives. This uncertainty can create tension within organisations, as decision-makers may prioritise short-term projects with clearer returns over long-term, exploratory innovation. Leaders must demonstrate the strategic value of innovation spending by showing how these investments contribute to sustained growth, adaptability, and competitive advantage.

Furthermore, budget allocation for innovation requires an adaptable approach to financial planning. Traditional budgeting often operates on annual cycles with fixed allocations, yet innovation is an evolving process that may require additional funding mid-cycle. Leaders must be prepared to advocate for flexible budgets or contingency funds to allow for real-time adjustments. Additionally, introducing metrics to measure innovation outcomes, such as customer feedback on new products or market impact, can help justify continued investment. Establishing innovation as a core priority within financial planning communicates its value to the organisation, fostering a proactive approach to long-term investment in transformative growth.

Another critical aspect of budget allocation for innovation is the challenge of balancing between incremental improvements and breakthrough initiatives. Incremental innovation—small, continuous improvements to existing products or processes—often offers a clearer path to ROI, making it easier to secure funding. However, breakthrough innovations, which introduce entirely new offerings or disrupt markets, are less predictable but have the potential for high rewards. Leaders must decide how much to allocate to each type, a decision that depends on the organisation's risk tolerance, market position, and long-term strategic vision. Often, a balanced portfolio approach is most effective, with a mix of low-risk incremental innovations and high-risk, high-reward breakthroughs.

Allocating funds also requires a method for assessing and prioritising innovative ideas, which can be challenging without standardised evaluation criteria. Organisations may implement internal 'innovation scoring' frameworks to rank ideas based on factors like potential impact, feasibility, alignment with strategic goals, and projected ROI. Such frameworks help justify budgets for innovation by providing decision-makers with quantitative data to compare ideas. Moreover, setting up a stage-gate funding model, where funds are released in phases based on the achievement of specific milestones, can provide a way to control spending and reduce risk. This phased approach enables organisations to commit to innovation while remaining flexible and responsive to early results, adjusting investments as necessary.

Bureaucratic Barriers

Bureaucratic barriers in innovation refer to the structures and processes within an organisation that create obstacles to creative thinking, risk-taking, and rapid decision-making. These barriers are often a result of rigid hierarchies, excessive approval processes, and a top-down management style that stifles autonomy and discourages experimentation. In bureaucratic organisations, decisions can take an extended amount of time due to the need for multiple layers of approval or consultation. As a result, ideas often lose their momentum before they can be fully explored or implemented. This slow pace of decision-making can be especially detrimental to innovation, where speed and agility are critical for success in dynamic markets.

One of the key factors that contribute to bureaucratic barriers is the centralisation of power. In highly bureaucratic organisations, decision-making authority is concentrated at the top levels of management, which limits the autonomy of middle management or frontline employees to make important decisions. This top-down approach often leads to a lack of ownership and accountability among employees, making them hesitant to propose or act on innovative ideas. Additionally, the need for approval from multiple layers of management can result in a loss of momentum, where projects that could have been successful are delayed or cancelled due to bureaucracy.

Another barrier is the emphasis on adherence to established processes and procedures, which can be a natural byproduct of a bureaucratic structure. While standardised processes are necessary for operational efficiency, they can become restrictive when it comes to innovation. Creative solutions often require flexibility and adaptability, yet bureaucratic organisations are often slow to change their existing methods or embrace new technologies. Employees may find it difficult to propose unconventional ideas if they do not align with the company's established norms or protocols. Over time, this focus on conformity can lead to a culture that resists change and discourages employees from challenging the status quo.

Lastly, bureaucratic barriers can be reinforced by a fear of failure or a risk-averse mentality. In organisations with heavy bureaucracy, employees and managers alike may be reluctant to pursue innovative initiatives due to the potential consequences of failure. The focus on maintaining control and minimising risk can make it difficult for leaders to support new ideas or experimental projects. Innovation, however, often requires a certain level of risk-taking and the ability to learn from failures. In a highly bureaucratic environment, where failure is often viewed negatively, employees may feel disincentivised to take the bold steps necessary for breakthrough innovations, further hindering the company's ability to stay competitive.

Success Stories of Companies Dealing With Innovation Issues

Microsoft – Cultural Transformation for Cloud Innovation

Microsoft provides a well-known example of a company overcoming resistance to change through a shift in organisational culture. When Satya Nadella became CEO in 2014, he faced substantial internal resistance to the company's pivot toward cloud computing and a more open, collaborative development environment. Many employees were accustomed to the traditional Windows-centric business model, and the shift to cloud and cross-platform services required a significant mindset change. Nadella championed a 'growth mindset' culture that encouraged learning, flexibility, and cross-departmental collaboration. Through transparent communication and a commitment to employee development, Microsoft's leadership helped staff embrace change, ultimately transforming the company into a leader in cloud computing through Azure. Today, Microsoft's success in cloud technology exemplifies the positive impact of reducing resistance to change through cultural transformation.

Under Nadella's leadership, Microsoft implemented several specific initiatives to encourage a growth mindset and reduce resistance to change. One of the foundational shifts was his emphasis on empathy and inclusivity, a marked change from the competitive culture that had previously characterised Microsoft. Nadella encouraged managers and employees to seek a deeper understanding of customer needs, prioritise teamwork, and embrace diverse perspectives across departments. This emphasis on empathy fostered a collaborative environment where employees felt more open to embracing new ideas and experimenting with innovative solutions.

Another critical strategy was Microsoft's investment in learning and development programs to help employees gain the skills needed for a cloud-focussed future. Nadella introduced the concept of 'learn-it-alls' rather than 'know-it-alls,' encouraging continuous learning rather than rigid expertise. This shift was supported by access to extensive training resources on cloud technologies, data analytics, and AI, which helped employees feel empowered and equipped to contribute to Microsoft's new direction. Employees were not only encouraged to upskill but were also given the resources and time to do so, which eased anxiety around adapting to the company's evolving technological focus. This investment in skill-building was essential in reducing resistance, as employees felt more confident in their ability to succeed within the new cloud ecosystem.

Additionally, Nadella's leadership made transparency a priority, with regular company-wide meetings and updates on Microsoft's strategy and progress in cloud computing. By openly discussing the rationale behind the shift to cloud services, Nadella fostered trust and built buy-in at all levels of the organisation. The emphasis on transparency allowed employees to see how their roles fit into the broader mission and how cloud computing would support Microsoft's long-term goals. This clarity around purpose and the role of each team member was key to overcoming resistance, as employees could align their work with the company's vision. Today, Microsoft's thriving cloud division, Azure, is a testament to the power of cultural transformation in overcoming resistance and positioning the company as a modern tech leader.

General Electric (GE) – Lean Budgeting

General Electric implemented the 'Fast Works' initiative to manage budget allocation for innovation effectively. Using principles from lean startup methodologies, GE adopted a customer-focussed, agile approach to innovation, where projects are developed in small, testable increments. This incremental process allows GE to allocate budgets in smaller chunks, avoiding large upfront investments and reducing the financial risk associated with uncertain outcomes. Fast Works helped GE launch products faster and at a lower cost, particularly in high-tech and industrial sectors, by focusing on rapid prototyping and iterative development (Goldstein & Euchner, 2017) (Kapoor et al., 2023).

The Fast Works initiative at GE transformed the company's approach to innovation by adopting a lean and agile framework traditionally associated with startups. In a field where large-scale, long-term projects are common, GE saw the need for faster, more flexible development cycles to remain competitive. The Fast

Works initiative empowers project teams to validate ideas and build prototypes with a focus on customer feedback rather than relying solely on internal assessments. By releasing early versions of products, testing in the real world, and iterating based on customer responses, GE minimises the risk of over-investing in ideas that may not resonate with the market. This agile process enables the company to shift resources quickly toward promising innovations without waiting for a complete overhaul.

Another core element of GE's lean budgeting approach is cross-functional collaboration. Fast Works teams are intentionally composed of members from various departments, such as engineering, marketing, and finance, allowing for a holistic view of each project's needs. This collaboration reduces budget misalignment by ensuring all stakeholders understand and support the project's direction from the outset. It also streamlines decision-making by breaking down traditional silos, helping the company respond to changes or setbacks more swiftly. The transparency of costs and goals across these cross-functional teams ensures that each project's financial requirements are met in a realistic, manageable way, avoiding the pitfalls of excess budget allocation.

Fast Works has also fostered a cultural shift within GE, where the focus is on learning and adapting rather than sticking rigidly to initial plans. The company encourages project teams to embrace a 'fail fast, learn faster' mindset, where early failures are seen as valuable learning opportunities rather than setbacks. This reduces the stigma associated with budget adjustments mid-project, as teams are empowered to reallocate resources based on real-time insights. By creating a culture where adaptive budgeting is the norm, GE not only optimises its spending but also maintains a competitive edge in the rapidly changing industrial and tech landscape. This strategic flexibility has enabled GE to respond to market demands more effectively, focusing its resources on innovations that truly meet customer needs.

Citi Ventures – Dedicated Innovation Teams to Avoid Bureaucratic Barriers

Citi, a global financial services company, created Citi Ventures to sidestep the bureaucratic constraints that often come with corporate management layers. Citi Ventures operates as a semi-autonomous division, specifically focussed on exploring and testing new technologies, such as blockchain, AI, and fintech innovations. This setup allows the division to work with external partners and startups while reducing the need for continual oversight from traditional management. Citi Ventures was designed to be free of the typical corporate hierarchy, giving its teams the flexibility to move quickly and respond to market opportunities. Although senior management initially hesitated to provide full autonomy, Citi Ventures' success in driving innovation and discovering new growth avenues helped overcome that resistance, allowing Citi to remain competitive in the fast-evolving fintech landscape.

To further combat frozen management, Citi Ventures established an innovation ecosystem that bridges the gap between traditional banking operations and emerging technologies. Citi Ventures' model was built around a corporate venture capital arm that invests in startups and disruptive technologies. This allowed the company to create external partnerships with tech firms, fintech startups, and other innovators while remaining nimble and adaptable. By working with external innovators, Citi Ventures was able to bring fresh ideas into the organisation, bypassing the traditional internal resistance to change. The innovation teams could experiment with new technologies like blockchain, AI, and machine learning, testing them in real-world scenarios without being bogged down by corporate bureaucracy.

Citi Ventures also implemented a 'fail-fast' mentality, where teams are encouraged to experiment rapidly and pivot quickly if an innovation does not meet expectations. This approach was crucial in overcoming management resistance, as it demonstrated that failure was part of the learning and innovation process rather than something to be feared or avoided. Managers who were initially hesitant about new and untested technologies soon saw that Citi Ventures' projects provided valuable learning experiences that could be applied across the broader organisation. This agile mindset helped break down the 'frozen management' barriers as leaders became more open to experimentation and risk-taking.

Moreover, Citi Ventures fosters an entrepreneurial culture that contrasts with the typical conservative, risk-averse mindset often found in large financial institutions. Through internal workshops, leadership development programs, and a focus on cross-functional collaboration, Citi Ventures encouraged employees to think like entrepreneurs. This culture of entrepreneurship empowered Citi's staff at all levels to take ownership of projects and contribute ideas without the approval chains that usually slow down decision-making in more traditional management structures. As the innovations began to gain traction, this culture shift within the organisation led to broader support for disruptive technologies, ultimately enabling Citi to remain at the forefront of digital banking and financial technology innovation.

The success of Citi Ventures has not only helped the company navigate the complexities of modern banking but also positioned Citi as a key player in the evolving landscape of fintech. By creating an environment where innovation could thrive independently of corporate red tape, Citi Ventures demonstrated how overcoming frozen management can lead to significant strategic advantages. This model has since been replicated by other financial institutions seeking to innovate and stay competitive in an increasingly digital world.

Chapter 7: Innovation Management

Innovation management is the systematic approach organisations use to foster, manage, and implement new ideas, processes, and technologies that lead to improvement or value creation. The goal is to enhance the company's competitive edge, increase customer satisfaction, streamline operations, or open new market opportunities. It's about more than just generating ideas—effective innovation management aligns innovations with business goals and structures the process of bringing these ideas to life.

Key principles of innovation management include:

1. **Strategic Alignment**: Innovation efforts should align with the organisation's strategic objectives. This alignment ensures that resources, focus, and time are dedicated to projects that will help achieve broader goals, whether that means expanding market share, improving product quality, or enhancing customer experiences.

2. **Customer-Centric Approach**: Successful innovation often stems from a deep understanding of customer needs, challenges, and desires. Innovating with the end-user in mind helps create products, services, or processes that truly resonate with the market and solve real-world problems.

3. **Empowering Culture**: An organisational culture that supports experimentation, risk-taking, and creativity is crucial. Employees should feel encouraged to share their ideas and explore novel solutions without fear of failure. This involves leadership buy-in, open communication, and sometimes even creating dedicated innovation teams or labs.

4. **Agility and Flexibility**: The ability to pivot quickly in response to feedback, new information, or changes in the market environment is essential. An agile approach allows organisations to iterate on ideas, test prototypes, and scale up successful innovations rapidly.

5. **Cross-Functional Collaboration**: Innovation often requires diverse perspectives and expertise. Facilitating collaboration between departments such as R&D, marketing, and customer service enables the integration of various insights, leading to more holistic solutions and faster development.

6. **Systematic Process**: A structured process for idea generation, evaluation, and implementation increases the likelihood of successful innovation. This can include idea management platforms, structured brainstorming sessions, stage-gate processes, and metrics for tracking progress and impact.

7. **Commitment to Continuous Improvement**: Innovation is not a one-time effort but an ongoing process. Embracing continuous improvement means that the organisation consistently seeks out ways to evolve and refine its processes, products, and

business models to stay ahead.

8. Balanced Portfolio of Innovation Types: Effective innovation management involves a mix of different types of innovation, such as incremental (small improvements), breakthrough (significant advancements), and disruptive (market-changing). Balancing these types can help an organization maintain stability while also positioning itself for long-term growth.

Innovation management, therefore, requires both a clear strategy and a supportive environment where creativity and experimentation can thrive. This approach ensures that innovative ideas are not only generated but also effectively refined, evaluated, and brought to market.

Detail Explanation and Example of Implementing the Principles

1. Strategic Alignment

Strategic alignment in innovation management ensures that innovation efforts directly contribute to an organisation's long-term goals and vision. Without alignment, innovation can become disjointed, and efforts might be wasted on ideas that do not fit the organization's mission or market direction. A company's innovation strategy should be rooted in its business strategy, making innovation not just a random act but a calculated pursuit that drives competitive advantage and organisational growth. Aligning innovation to strategy also allows the company to prioritise initiatives, allocate resources effectively, and track the value generated by innovations.

For example, when Apple launched the iPhone, it wasn't just about creating a new phone; it was about integrating a phone with an MP3 player, a camera, and an internet browser, effectively redefining the mobile industry. This strategic alignment with Apple's long-term goal of transforming consumer electronics and enhancing the user experience was key to its success. By aligning innovation with its brand's mission and consumer expectations, Apple was able to create a revolutionary product that captured the market's attention.

Moreover, strategic alignment helps organisations focus their innovation efforts on projects that have the highest potential return on investment. If an organisation aims to become a market leader in sustainable technology, innovations that reduce carbon footprints or promote renewable energy are prioritised. In contrast, if the goal is cost leadership, innovations in process efficiency or automation take precedence.

To ensure alignment, companies must establish clear channels of communication between leadership and innovation teams, ensuring everyone understands the business priorities. Regular reviews of the innovation portfolio are also necessary to assess whether each project is still aligned with the firm's evolving strategy.

Finally, alignment also means being adaptable. As business strategies evolve based on market changes or new opportunities, innovation efforts must be flexible enough to adjust. For instance, a company may shift its focus from purely product innovations to digital transformation initiatives as market demand changes and innovation management must support this pivot.

2. Customer-Centric Approach

The foundation of successful innovation is understanding customer needs, preferences, and pain points. A customer-centric approach ensures that new ideas solve real problems and provide tangible benefits to the target audience. This principle encourages companies to look beyond internal capabilities and instead focus on the external market—what customers value most, how they behave, and what challenges they face. By using customer feedback, data analysis, and direct engagement, businesses can tailor innovations to meet specific demands and improve the customer experience.

Consider how Netflix revolutionised entertainment consumption by focusing on the customer experience. Initially a DVD rental service, Netflix transitioned to streaming and introduced personalised content recommendations based on customer viewing history. By aligning innovation with customer preferences, the company reshaped the media landscape, providing a highly engaging, on-demand platform that responded to the growing demand for convenience and choice. The organisation's ability to evolve in response to customer expectations led to its dominance in the entertainment industry.

Firms can also use tools such as surveys, user testing, and market research to gather insights about what customers need and value. This feedback loop helps businesses identify trends, validate ideas, and prioritise innovations that will most effectively impact customers. A customer-centric approach doesn't just apply to product development but can also extend to customer service, marketing strategies, and the overall user journey.

For example, in the tech industry, companies like Amazon and Apple have set the standard for customer-centric innovation. Amazon's obsession with customer experience has led to innovations like Prime, one-click purchasing, and Alexa, all designed to make shopping easier and more personalised for customers. Similarly, Apple's focus on seamless integration across its products ensures that users have a consistent, intuitive experience across devices.

Finally, customer-centric innovation encourages continuous feedback and iteration. Businesses need to remain agile, adapting to shifting customer expectations or changing market dynamics. This ongoing engagement allows companies to refine their products or services and stay ahead of the competition.

3. Empowering Culture

An empowering culture is critical to fostering innovation, as it encourages employees to think creatively, experiment, and take risks. In such a culture, failure is seen as an opportunity for learning rather than a setback, allowing individuals to freely explore ideas without the fear of repercussions. Innovation thrives in environments where diverse teams collaborate, share knowledge, and challenge each other's thinking. Leadership plays a pivotal role in creating this culture by demonstrating a commitment to innovation, celebrating new ideas, and removing bureaucratic hurdles that stifle creativity.

One of the best examples of a company with an empowering culture is Google. Google's famous "20% time" initiative allowed employees to spend one day a week working on personal projects, leading to the creation of groundbreaking products like Gmail and Google News. By empowering employees to pursue their passions and take ownership of innovative ideas, the company created a culture where creativity could flourish.

Building an empowering culture requires establishing trust between leadership and staff. Leaders must encourage open communication, reward initiative, and provide resources for idea development. This sense of empowerment helps employees feel they can contribute meaningfully to the organisation's success, which in turn fuels innovation. It also requires a willingness to support ideas that may not have an immediate return on investment but could lead to significant breakthroughs down the line.

An empowering culture also requires diversity—diverse teams bring varied perspectives, experiences, and expertise that enrich the ideation process. For instance, at companies like IDEO, diverse teams collaborate to solve design challenges, resulting in innovative solutions that may not have emerged in a more homogeneous group. Diversity of thought is essential for creativity and helps organisations tackle problems from multiple angles.

Finally, an empowering culture is sustainable only when it is consistently nurtured. Organisations should offer training and development programs that encourage innovation, foster leadership at all levels, and maintain an open, collaborative environment where new ideas can flourish. By continuously reinforcing these values, companies can ensure a steady stream of innovation.

4. Agility and Flexibility

Agility and flexibility in innovation management mean the ability to quickly adapt to changing circumstances, market conditions, or customer needs. Innovation is rarely a linear process; instead, it is iterative, involving frequent revisions and adaptations. Companies that embrace agility in their innovation practices can rapidly test and refine new ideas, products, or processes, ensuring they stay relevant and competitive. This flexibility is particularly crucial in fast-paced industries like technology, where disruptions happen frequently, and being slow to adapt can result in lost opportunities.

A good example of agility in innovation is seen in the way software companies develop products using agile. For instance, companies like Microsoft and Atlassian rely on agile frameworks to release software updates regularly, making incremental improvements based on user feedback. This iterative approach allows them to address issues quickly, add features in response to customer requests, and improve user experience over time.

Flexibility also means that businesses are willing to pivot when necessary. A well-known example is Twitter, which started as a podcasting platform called Odeo before realizing that microblogging was a more promising market. The team pivoted quickly and launched Twitter, which eventually became one of the world's largest social media platforms. This ability to shift focus when new opportunities arise is a key aspect of an agile innovation strategy.

To maintain agility, organisations need a flexible structure that enables fast decision-making and rapid execution. This includes having smaller, cross-functional teams that can move quickly without being bogged down by rigid hierarchies or lengthy approval processes. It also means implementing systems that allow teams to gather and analyse customer data in real-time so they can make informed decisions about what to change or improve.

Lastly, agility in innovation management allows for learning from failure. When an innovation doesn't work as planned, agile organisations treat it as an opportunity to refine the approach, learn from the mistakes, and continue evolving. This iterative learning process is crucial for continuous innovation and ensures that the organisation can keep improving even when things don't go according to plan.

5. Balanced Portfolio of Innovation Types

A balanced portfolio of innovation types involves managing a mix of incremental, breakthrough, and disruptive innovations. Incremental innovations improve existing products or processes, breakthrough innovations introduce new concepts that significantly advance the field, and disruptive innovations create entirely new markets or disrupt existing ones. A well-balanced innovation portfolio ensures that organisations continue to innovate in ways that improve current offerings while also positioning themselves for future growth.

For example, in the automotive industry, Tesla has balanced incremental innovation with disruptive innovation. While the company continuously improves its electric vehicles (incremental innovation), it also pioneers new approaches to autonomous driving and energy storage, positioning itself as a leader in the future of transportation (disruptive innovation). Tesla's innovation portfolio is a mix of both steady improvements to existing technologies and ambitious leaps into new frontiers.

Companies like 3M have also perfected this balance. 3M consistently invests in incremental innovations across its product lines (e.g., improving adhesive products) while simultaneously funding breakthrough innovations like new healthcare solutions and cutting-edge materials. By diversifying the types of innovation

111

in its portfolio, the company maintains a competitive edge across multiple industries.

A well-balanced innovation portfolio also helps mitigate risk. Focusing exclusively on breakthrough or disruptive innovation can be high-risk, as these innovations are harder to predict and require significant resources. On the other hand, incremental innovations may not always offer the competitive advantage necessary to stay ahead of the competition. By balancing these types, companies can manage risk while positioning themselves for long-term success.

Finally, managing a balanced innovation portfolio requires continuous assessment and adjustment. As market conditions change, an organisation may need to shift its focus from incremental to more disruptive innovations or vice versa. Regular portfolio reviews ensure that the organisation's innovation strategy is always in line with current market trends and long-term objectives.

ISO Innovation Management

What Is ISO Innovation Management?

ISO Innovation Management refers to the guidelines and standards set by the International Organization for Standardization (ISO) to help organisations systematically manage innovation. The most well-known standard in this area is ISO 56000, which outlines the framework and principles for innovation management. ISO 56000 provides organisations with a structured approach to creating, developing, and sustaining innovations across all levels.

It offers guidance on how to integrate innovation practices into an organisation's management processes, from strategic planning to the implementation of new products, services, or processes.

The ISO 56000 series is designed to be flexible and applicable to a wide range of industries, from manufacturing to technology to service sectors. It's not a one-size-fits-all approach but a comprehensive set of guidelines that can be tailored to the specific needs and maturity level of an organisation. ISO Innovation Management provides organisations with a common language and set of standards for innovation, helping them ensure that their innovation processes are consistent, repeatable, and measurable.

In practice, ISO Innovation Management encourages organisations to approach innovation in a structured way, establishing clear roles, responsibilities, and processes. It helps businesses move beyond ad-hoc or sporadic innovation efforts and fosters a culture where innovation is seen as an integral part of the organisation's strategy and operations. By following ISO standards, companies can achieve greater alignment between innovation efforts and business objectives, ensuring that innovations lead to tangible outcomes.

ISO 56000 focuses on the management of innovation at various levels, including organisational culture, strategic goals, processes, and performance metrics. It encourages companies to create an innovation management system (IMS) that is continuously reviewed and improved. This continuous improvement process is key to ensuring that innovation remains a driving force within the organisation rather than a one-time initiative or isolated project.

Finally, ISO Innovation Management emphasises the importance of leadership and organisational support. It encourages top management to take responsibility for promoting innovation throughout the organisation and for creating an environment that fosters creativity and risk-taking. This ensures that innovation is not only an individual effort but a collective organisational priority.

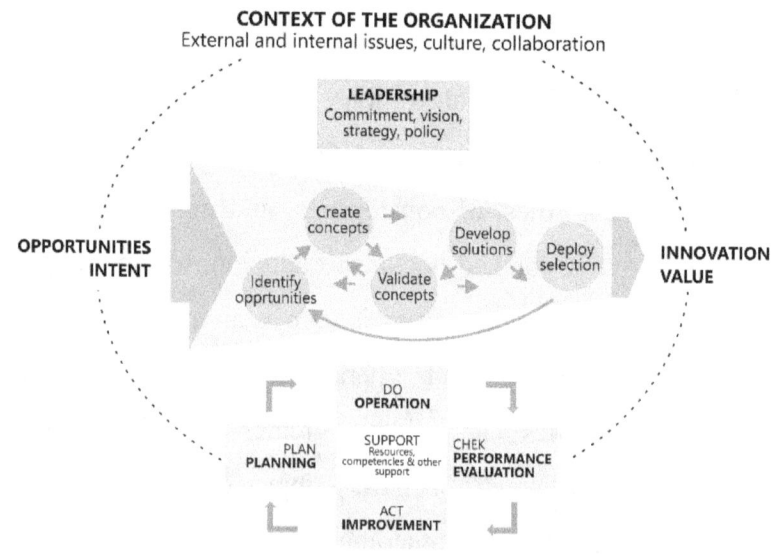

Source: adjusted from viima.com

Why ISO Innovation Management?

Adopting ISO Innovation Management brings numerous benefits to organisations, particularly in terms of ensuring that innovation is strategically integrated, scalable, and sustainable. In an increasingly competitive global market, innovation is a key differentiator, and the ISO framework helps businesses stay ahead of the curve by providing a clear and structured approach. The standard enables companies to manage innovation more effectively, align it with business objectives, and measure its impact, leading to more successful outcomes.

One major advantage of implementing ISO 56000 is the enhanced consistency it brings to innovation efforts. Without a formalised approach, innovation can become fragmented, with different teams pursuing disconnected or redundant ideas. By following ISO guidelines, organisations can streamline their innovation processes, ensuring that all efforts contribute toward a shared goal and align with the company's overall strategic vision. This consistency also facilitates better collaboration between departments, making innovation a more cohesive and integrated part of the company culture.

Moreover, ISO Innovation Management supports organisations in identifying and mitigating risks associated with innovation. Innovation inherently carries uncertainties, and without proper management, it can lead to wasted resources or failure to meet market needs. ISO provides tools for managing this risk by encouraging thorough evaluation, testing, and monitoring of innovation initiatives. This helps businesses focus on the most promising ideas and reduce the likelihood of costly mistakes or missteps in the innovation process.

Implementing ISO standards also enhances an organisation's credibility and reputation. ISO certifications are globally recognised, and demonstrating adherence to ISO 56000 signals to customers, partners, and investors that the organisation is committed to continuous improvement and is actively working to innovate in a structured, effective manner. This credibility can improve relationships with stakeholders, boost customer confidence, and open up new business opportunities.

Furthermore, ISO Innovation Management facilitates the measurement and tracking of innovation performance. The standards offer guidance on how to define key performance indicators (KPIs) and other metrics to assess the effectiveness of innovation initiatives. By measuring success, organisations can identify areas for improvement, ensure that innovation efforts are contributing to business goals, and justify investments in innovation to stakeholders.

Key Components of ISO Innovation Management

ISO Innovation Management is composed of several key components that help organisations create a comprehensive and sustainable innovation management system. These components guide the development, implementation, and assessment of innovation processes at various levels of the organization. One of the core elements is the need for leadership commitment. Leaders must be fully invested in the innovation process and actively promote a culture that supports creative thinking, experimentation, and continuous improvement.

Another critical component is the establishment of an innovation strategy. This strategy defines the organisation's approach to innovation, aligning it with overall business objectives and identifying the focus areas where innovation can have the greatest impact. The strategy also provides the framework for decision-making, helping to prioritise which innovation projects to pursue based on their potential value and alignment with organisational goals.

The ISO framework also highlights the importance of creating a conducive environment for innovation. This involves fostering a culture of openness, collaboration, and risk-taking. It encourages organisations to remove barriers that hinder innovation, such as bureaucratic processes, and to create structures that support creativity and experimentation. Innovation processes should be flexible and adaptable, allowing teams to respond to changes in the market or technology swiftly and effectively.

Collaboration is another key aspect emphasized by ISO Innovation Management. Innovation is rarely the result of individual efforts; it requires cross-functional teamwork and the integration of different perspectives. ISO 56000 encourages organisations to promote collaboration across departments, creating multidisciplinary teams that can tackle challenges from multiple angles. This approach maximises the potential for breakthrough innovations and increases the chances of success in the market.

Finally, ISO Innovation Management stresses the importance of continuous learning and improvement. Organisations are encouraged to assess and refine their innovation management processes regularly. This involves collecting data on innovation performance, analysing successes and failures, and making necessary adjustments to improve outcomes. Continuous improvement helps ensure that innovation remains a core capability of the organisation and can evolve in response to new challenges and opportunities.

ISO Innovation Management Process

The ISO 56000 series outlines a structured process for managing innovation from inception to implementation. This process includes several stages, each designed to ensure that ideas are thoroughly evaluated, developed, and deployed in a way that adds value to the organisation. The first stage involves idea generation, where firms actively encourage employees, customers, and other stakeholders to submit ideas for improvement or new products. During this phase, companies need to ensure that the idea-generation process is inclusive and diverse, tapping into a wide range of sources for innovation.

Once ideas are generated, the next phase focuses on selecting the most promising ones. This is where the strategic alignment of innovation with business objectives comes into play. Using the criteria defined in the innovation strategy, ideas are assessed for their feasibility, market potential, and alignment with the company's long-term goals. The selection process often involves collaboration across different departments to ensure that the chosen ideas have broad support and are viable from technical, financial, and customer perspectives.

After selecting ideas, the development phase begins, which is where the innovation is brought to life. This phase involves prototyping, testing, and refining the idea, often in an iterative manner. It requires collaboration between various departments, including R&D, marketing, finance, and operations, to ensure the innovation meets customer needs and is feasible within the company's operational constraints. Testing and validation are critical at this stage to avoid costly mistakes or product failures.

Once an innovation has been developed and refined, it enters the implementation phase, where it is launched to the market or integrated into the company's operations. This stage involves the final rollout, marketing, distribution, and customer support. It is essential to monitor the performance of the innovation after implementation to assess its success and gather feedback from users for further refinement.

Finally, the ISO Innovation Management process involves continuous evaluation and learning. Post-launch reviews and performance assessments are conducted to understand the impact of the innovation and identify areas for improvement. This feedback loop is critical to ensuring that innovation processes remain effective and that lessons learned are applied to future innovation projects.

The Benefits of ISO Innovation Management

Adopting ISO Innovation Management can bring a multitude of benefits to organisations, particularly in terms of improving their innovation capabilities, increasing efficiency, and driving long-term growth. One of the most significant benefits is the improvement in organisational focus. By aligning innovation activities with business strategy, businesses can prioritize high-value innovations and direct resources to the areas that matter most. This focus helps avoid wasted efforts on irrelevant or low-impact ideas, improving overall productivity and innovation success rates.

Additionally, the systematic approach offered by ISO Innovation Management helps organisations manage innovation risks more effectively. Innovation often involves uncertainty, but by following the ISO framework, companies can evaluate, test, and measure new ideas before committing significant resources. This structured risk management approach ensures that innovations are carefully vetted, reducing the likelihood of costly failures and increasing the chances of successful outcomes.

ISO Innovation Management also drives greater accountability within the organisation. By establishing clear roles, responsibilities, and performance metrics, the framework ensures that everyone involved in the innovation process understands their contribution and is held accountable for outcomes. This clarity helps streamline the decision-making process and ensures that innovation activities are properly coordinated across departments.

The credibility and recognition that come with ISO certification are also valuable advantages. Being ISO-certified demonstrates to customers, partners, and stakeholders that an organisation is committed to managing innovation in a professional and effective manner. It strengthens trust in the company's ability to deliver innovative products or services, which can improve customer loyalty, attract new business, and open doors to strategic partnerships.

Finally, ISO Innovation Management promotes a culture of continuous improvement. Organisations that follow the ISO framework regularly assess and refine their innovation practices, leading to better outcomes over time. By embedding innovation into the company's DNA and ensuring it is always evolving, ISO helps organisations stay competitive, adaptable, and prepared for future challenges.

The Innovation Process: Utilising a Design Thinking Approach

What Is Design Thinking?

Design thinking is an iterative, human-centred approach to problem-solving that emphasises empathy, experimentation, and collaboration. This process begins by deeply understanding the users' needs and challenges, framing the problem with a human-centred perspective. Through structured brainstorming and ideation sessions, designers and innovators can explore diverse solutions, which are then developed into prototypes for real-world testing. This feedback-driven approach encourages constant refinement, ensuring that solutions evolve to better meet user needs and ultimately drive impactful change.

Design thinking's unique integration of analytical and creative faculties is a key strength. This methodology encourages individuals to explore divergent possibilities and converge on feasible solutions, balancing imaginative ideation with rigorous assessment of constraints and practical considerations. This multifaceted approach fosters well-rounded innovation, empowering teams to challenge assumptions, explore diverse perspectives, and move beyond conventional solutions. Such a comprehensive process is vital in addressing complex challenges that demand outcomes that are both effective and adaptable to real-world conditions.

In recent years, design thinking has grown significantly in influence across various fields. Originally rooted in product and industrial design, it has expanded into business strategy, social innovation, and even policy-making. By placing users and stakeholders at the centre, design thinking has shown success in developing solutions that are not only functional but also resonate with the end-users. This expansion demonstrates how powerful design thinking can be for creating lasting change in diverse areas, ranging from organisational change to global social issues.

Why Design Thinking?

In today's world, where complex and unpredictable problems have become the norm, design thinking offers a robust approach to navigating uncertainty and fostering creativity. Complex challenges, often referred to as "wicked problems," resist traditional problem-solving techniques due to their ill-structured nature and evolving parameters. Design thinking's reliance on iterative feedback and co-creation enables teams to explore unconventional ideas while maintaining a user-centred focus, reducing the risk of cognitive biases. This method helps organisations harness their collective creative potential, often leading to more innovative and impactful outcomes.

Design thinking is also valued for its versatility and adaptability, making it applicable across a broad spectrum of industries and practices. From startups seeking to disrupt markets with novel products to governments aiming to provide more effective public services, design thinking provides a toolkit for addressing challenges in ways that are more responsive to the needs of the end-user. The design thinking framework encourages empathy and user-focussed inquiry, which can significantly improve the relevance and effectiveness of solutions across sectors, including business, education, and the nonprofit domain.

Beyond tangible outcomes, design thinking also cultivates a culture of collaboration and inclusivity within teams. By involving diverse stakeholders and perspectives in the design process, organisations can foster an environment of shared purpose and open communication. This collaborative culture has been shown to enhance team dynamics, boost morale, and empower individuals to contribute their unique insights, ultimately leading to solutions that are both innovative and sustainable. As organisations continue to face rapid changes and evolving demands, design thinking's inclusive, iterative, and adaptive nature makes it a valuable approach for creating solutions that are meaningful and resilient.

Types of Design Thinking Methods

There are several design thinking frameworks that have been developed and utilized by practitioners and researchers.

Design Thinking Stanford Model

One of the most widely recognized models is the Design Thinking for Educators process developed by the Hasso Plattner Institute of Design at Stanford University, also known as the d.school.

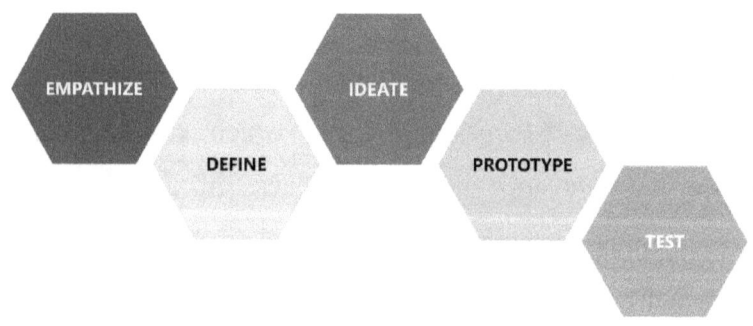

Source: Stanford d.school

The Stanford model is a widely used framework for tackling complex problems through a human-centred, iterative approach. It consists of five core stages: Empathise, Define, Ideate, Prototype, and Test. Each stage builds upon the previous one, guiding teams through a structured yet flexible process to deeply understand the problem, generate innovative ideas, and refine solutions based on feedback.

1. Empathise

The first stage, empathise, focusses on understanding the needs, motivations, and challenges of the people for whom a solution is being designed. This stage involves immersive research techniques, such as interviews, observations, and engaging directly with end-users to gain a comprehensive understanding of their experiences and emotions. By empathising with users, designers can identify pain points, uncover hidden needs, and set the foundation for a more meaningful solution. The empathize stage fosters a sense of connection between the design team and users, which is critical for developing truly user-centred solutions.

2. Define

In the define stage, insights gathered from the empathise phase are synthesized to form a clear problem statement. This involves organising and analysing data to reveal common patterns, insights, and themes, which help distil a complex array of user information into a focussed problem statement. Known as the "Point of View" (POV) statement, this definition represents the core challenge that needs solving, framed in a way that is actionable and user-centred. A well-articulated POV enables teams to stay focussed on addressing users' actual needs rather than perceived or assumed ones, guiding the ideation process effectively.

3. Ideate

Ideate is the stage where creativity is unleashed, allowing teams to brainstorm and generate a wide array of ideas that could potentially solve the defined problem. Here, designers are encouraged to think divergently, exploring as many possible solutions as they can without constraints or judgment. Techniques like brainstorming, mind mapping, and "crazy eights" (a rapid sketching exercise) are commonly used to expand the range of ideas. The goal of this stage is to go beyond conventional thinking, pushing boundaries to find unique approaches that could better meet users' needs. Once a broad range of ideas has been generated, the team can start narrowing down options to focus on the most promising solutions.

4. Prototype

In the prototype stage, selected ideas are turned into tangible, low-fidelity versions of the proposed solution. Prototypes can be anything from simple sketches, storyboards, or physical models to digital mock-ups, depending on the project's nature. The objective is to create a version of the product or experience that can be tested and interacted with by users, allowing the team to explore how effectively the solution addresses the problem. Prototyping encourages a mindset of "failing fast to succeed sooner," enabling teams to quickly identify and learn from weaknesses and refine their ideas.

5. Test

The final stage, test, involves presenting prototypes to users for feedback. This is a critical phase where the design team learns directly from users about what works, what doesn't, and why. Through observing user interactions, gathering feedback, and conducting interviews, the team gains valuable insights into how to improve the solution. Testing is often iterative, where multiple rounds of feedback lead to refinements and adjustments. Sometimes, testing can even lead back to earlier stages, prompting teams to redefine the problem or re-ideate based on newfound insights.

The Stanford design thinking model emphasises that the process is non-linear. Teams may cycle back through stages as new insights arise, allowing them to refine the solution continuously. This flexible, iterative approach is key to solving complex problems in a way that is deeply aligned with user needs.

Design Thinking IDEO

IDEO, one of the pioneering design and innovation firms, has popularised design thinking as a structured, human-centred approach to innovation. Their model emphasises empathy, collaboration, and experimentation, and it focuses on creating solutions that are desirable (human-centred), feasible (technologically possible), and viable (business-sustainable). IDEO's approach to design thinking is widely used across industries to solve complex challenges in creative, innovative ways. While the model is flexible and adaptable, IDEO generally structures its design thinking process around three main phases: Inspiration, Ideation, and Implementation.

IDEO Design Thingking Process

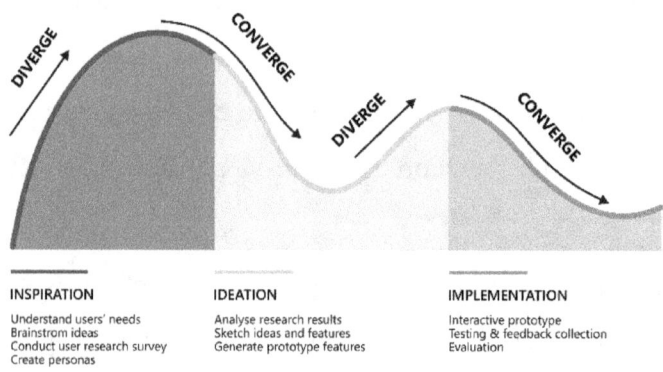

INSPIRATION
Understand users' needs
Brainstrom ideas
Conduct user research survey
Create personas

IDEATION
Analyse research results
Sketch ideas and features
Generate prototype features

IMPLEMENTATION
Interactive prototype
Testing & feedback collection
Evaluation

Source: RNF Technologies

1. Inspiration

Inspiration is the phase where the design team immerses itself in the lives and experiences of the end-users to deeply understand their needs, desires, and challenges. The goal here is to gain empathy and discover insights that may inform and guide the design process. IDEO encourages designers to conduct ethnographic research methods such as interviews, direct observations, and immersion into the user's environment. This immersion allows designers to uncover hidden, often unarticulated, needs that might not be immediately obvious. Inspiration is about gathering a diverse set of insights, breaking down preconceptions, and reframing the design challenge based on real user experiences.

A significant aspect of the inspiration phase at IDEO is the emphasis on storytelling. By capturing users' stories and emotions, designers can bring the problem to life and create a shared understanding among team members. This emotional connection forms the foundation for generating solutions that are not just functional but resonate deeply with the user.

2. Ideation

The ideation phase is where creativity and collaboration take centre stage. Based on the insights from the inspiration phase, the team begins brainstorming to generate a wide range of ideas and potential solutions. IDEO's philosophy promotes quantity over quality at this stage—encouraging as many ideas as possible, even if some seem unfeasible or "wild." IDEO often uses techniques like brainstorming sessions, sketching, and storyboarding to help teams visualise their ideas. In these sessions, team members are encouraged to build on each other's ideas and think without constraints, fostering a culture of open-mindedness and innovation.

IDEO values cross-disciplinary collaboration, bringing together people from various backgrounds, such as engineers, designers, psychologists, and business experts, to generate a diverse pool of ideas. By leveraging different perspectives, IDEO ensures that solutions are comprehensive and consider multiple aspects of the problem. At the end of the ideation phase, the team narrows down their ideas to a select few that hold the most promise, which are then prioritised for prototyping.

3. Implementation

The implementation phase focuses on bringing selected ideas to life through rapid prototyping and testing. IDEO advocates for creating simple, low-fidelity prototypes that allow the team to experiment, learn, and refine quickly. These prototypes can range from paper sketches to digital mock-ups or basic physical models, depending on the nature of the project. Prototyping is an essential component at IDEO because it encourages a "fail fast, learn faster" mentality, where ideas are continuously improved based on feedback. Testing these prototypes with real users allows the team to see how well the solution addresses the user's needs and identify areas for refinement.

As the solution is further developed, the team iterates based on user feedback and moves toward creating a final, high-fidelity version. IDEO's emphasis on iteration and flexibility means that even during implementation, the team may return to earlier stages (like ideation or even inspiration) if feedback reveals new insights or needs. This ensures that the final solution is well-aligned with the user's needs, feasible, and viable for implementation.

IDEO's Guiding Principles in Design Thinking

IDEO's approach is shaped by certain guiding principles. First, they emphasise a human-centred perspective, always designing with empathy and the user's experience in mind. Second, IDEO champions a bias toward action—rather than overanalysing, they prefer to get ideas out into the real world quickly to learn through doing. Finally, IDEO fosters a culture of collaboration and playfulness, encouraging designers to embrace creativity and openness, which are essential for innovation.

IDEO's guiding principles in design thinking emphasise a holistic approach to innovation that not only delivers solutions but also builds a mindset of continuous learning, empathy, and creativity. One of their key principles is the *human-centred approach,* which is foundational to all of IDEO's work. This principle asserts that all design decisions should be grounded in the understanding of real human experiences, needs, and motivations. IDEO believes that meaningful innovation starts with empathy, which is why their process heavily incorporates methods like ethnographic research and immersive user studies. By getting as close as possible to the user's perspective, IDEO designers can identify pain points and desires that may otherwise be overlooked, ensuring that solutions are deeply resonant and relevant.

Another guiding principle at IDEO is the idea of having a *bias toward action.* This principle encourages designers to quickly move from abstract ideas to tangible prototypes. IDEO emphasises the importance of "doing" rather than "debating," as they believe that taking ideas into the real world, even in rough forms, is the best way to test their effectiveness and feasibility. Prototyping allows the team to identify flaws early, make improvements, and gain insights faster than they would through theory alone. This action-oriented approach encourages a mindset of rapid experimentation, where even "failed" prototypes are seen as learning opportunities that bring the team closer to an effective solution.

IDEO also fosters a culture of *collaboration* and interdisciplinary teamwork, recognising that innovation is best achieved when multiple perspectives come together. Their teams are deliberately composed of people from varied backgrounds—engineers, anthropologists, business experts, and more—to ensure that solutions are well-rounded and take into account different angles and expertise. This collaborative environment helps break down silos and encourages open, constructive dialogue, allowing ideas to evolve through input from all team members. IDEO's collaborative ethos also extends to involving clients and users in the design process, creating a shared sense of ownership, and ensuring that the final solution meets real needs.

Creativity and *playfulness* are also essential principles in IDEO's design thinking process. IDEO encourages a workplace culture where experimentation and open-mindedness are celebrated, helping designers stay inspired and open to unconventional ideas. The playful element isn't just about having fun; it serves as a powerful tool for fostering a fearless, flexible approach to problem-solving, where even the most "out-there" ideas are welcome and often lead to surprising breakthroughs. Playfulness helps the team avoid taking assumptions too seriously and allows them to embrace "what if" questions, leading to innovative solutions that might not emerge from more rigid or risk-averse mindsets.

Finally, IDEO is committed to *iteration,* which underscores the importance of viewing solutions as evolving entities rather than finished products. The iterative process allows solutions to be refined continuously as they move through various stages of user testing and feedback. IDEO sees iteration not as a series of corrections but as an integral part of the design process that brings each solution closer to an ideal fit with user needs. This principle of iteration reflects IDEO's belief in lifelong learning and adaptability, fostering a dynamic design process that can adapt to changing requirements and emerging insights, ultimately producing solutions that are not only effective but also sustainable and resilient in real-world contexts.

Double Diamond Design Thinking

The Double Diamond model of design thinking, developed by the UK's Design Council, is a visual representation of the design process that emphasizes exploration, divergence, and convergence.

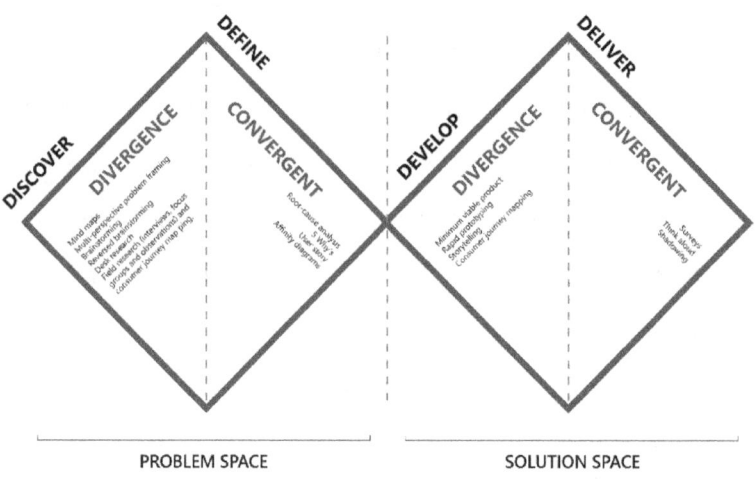

Source: www.designorate.com

It consists of two main stages, each shaped like a diamond: *discover and define* (the first diamond) and *develop and deliver* (the second diamond). The double diamond structure illustrates the process of expanding and narrowing down ideas to arrive at user-centred solutions that are both feasible and impactful.

1. Discover

The first phase, discover, is where the design team begins by *diverging*—exploring as many aspects of the problem as possible to gain a deep understanding of the context and the users. This phase involves extensive research to identify users' needs, behaviours, and challenges. Methods such as ethnographic studies, interviews, observations, and market research are commonly used to gather rich insights about the problem space. The goal of the discover phase is to look beyond assumptions and gain a fresh, unbiased perspective on the problem. By thoroughly exploring the environment and experiences of users, the team can identify underlying issues and unmet needs that will inform the design process.

2. Define

After gathering insights in the discover phase, the next step is the define phase, where the team *converges* by synthesising their research findings into a clear problem statement. In this phase, the team organises, categorises, and analyses the data to reveal patterns, insights, and themes that clarify what users truly need. This stage often involves creating "How Might We" (HMW) statements or other frameworks that focus the problem on actionable, user-centred goals. Defining the problem is crucial because it sets the direction for ideation and solution development. A well-articulated problem statement ensures that the team addresses the right challenge and remains aligned with users' needs.

3. Develop

The develop phase marks the beginning of the second diamond, where the team once again *diverges*, this time generating a wide array of ideas and potential solutions to the problem identified. In this phase, brainstorming, sketching, and other ideation techniques are employed to produce as many innovative ideas as possible. It's a creative exploration stage where designers are encouraged to think broadly and push beyond conventional solutions. After generating numerous ideas, the team selects the most promising concepts to develop into prototypes, allowing them to start testing their ideas in a tangible form. This phase emphasises experimentation and creativity, with the goal of exploring diverse approaches to solve the defined problem.

4. Deliver

In the final phase, deliver, the team *converges* once more, focusing on refining and implementing the best solutions. Prototypes created during the develop phase are tested, iterated, and optimised based on user feedback to ensure they are both functional and effective. The deliver phase includes multiple rounds of testing and iteration, allowing the design team to adjust the solution to better meet users' needs and eliminate any potential issues. By the end of this phase, the solution is ready to be finalised and launched. Deliver focuses on executing and delivering the final product or solution in a way that aligns with both user requirements and business objectives.

Key Takeaways of the Double Diamond Model

The Double Diamond model underscores the importance of moving back and forth between divergent (broad exploration) and convergent (focussed refinement) thinking throughout the design process. It highlights that effective problem-solving involves not only creating solutions but also defining the problem accurately and understanding it from multiple angles. By visualising the process in two "diamonds," the model demonstrates that both exploration and refinement are necessary for the journey to create meaningful, user-centred solutions.

Design Sprint: A Condensed Approach to Design Thinking

The Design Sprint is a structured, five-day process developed by Google Ventures (GV) that rapidly takes teams from identifying a problem to testing a prototype with real users. It's a condensed form of design thinking that emphasises speed, focus, and collaboration to quickly solve complex challenges. The sprint is designed to align teams, minimise risk, and efficiently test ideas before committing significant resources to development. The five-day sprint framework consists of five stages: Understand, Sketch, Decide, Prototype, and Test.

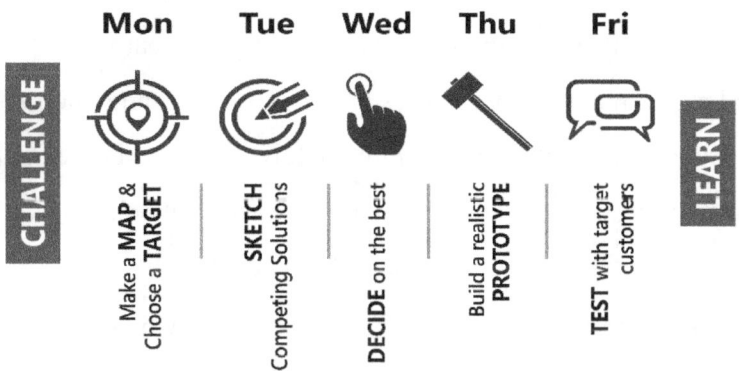

Source: adjusted from thesprintbook.com

1. Understand (Day 1)

The first day of a Design Sprint is all about building a comprehensive understanding of the problem the team is trying to solve. The day typically begins with presentations or discussions around existing research, insights, and relevant data. This shared information gives everyone a clear picture of the challenge from multiple angles. It's a time for team members to ask questions, challenge assumptions, and gather input from different perspectives. Techniques like expert interviews, competitor analysis, and examining previous user feedback can reveal crucial insights that might inform the direction of the sprint. By immersing themselves in the problem context, the team aligns on what success would look like at the end of the sprint.

This phase is also critical for framing the challenge effectively, often through the use of tools like user journey maps or "How Might We" (HMW) questions. Journey maps visualise the steps users take while interacting with the product or service, helping the team understand pain points and areas for potential improvement. HMW questions, on the other hand, allow the team to rephrase challenges in a way that invites creative thinking and encourages solutions that might not be immediately obvious. For example, "How might we make online shopping easier for seniors?" could unlock specific insights and ideas about accessibility.

The understand phase concludes with establishing clear goals and constraints, which define the boundaries for the rest of the sprint. Everyone in the team, including designers, developers, marketers, and stakeholders, aligns on the priorities and objectives, reducing miscommunication and ensuring a focussed effort throughout the week. By the end of Day 1, the team has set the stage for a structured, user-centred approach to the challenge, with a shared vision that will guide the subsequent stages.

2. Sketch (Day 2)

On the second day, the team transitions from understanding the problem to generating possible solutions. This phase is known as sketch, where each team member independently brainstorms and visualizes ideas, encouraging a diversity of concepts. To spark creativity, exercises like "Crazy 8s" are often employed. In Crazy 8s, each participant sketches eight different solutions in just eight minutes, pushing them to move quickly and avoid overthinking. This exercise helps surface unexpected ideas and encourages out-of-the-box thinking that might not arise in group discussions. The goal of the sketch phase is to produce a range of solutions that approach the problem in unique ways.

Unlike traditional brainstorming sessions, where individuals share ideas aloud, this phase is intentionally structured to foster independent ideation. By working solo, team members are not influenced by others' suggestions, which prevents groupthink and creates a broader selection of ideas. Each team member's perspective adds value, whether they're from design, engineering, or business backgrounds, leading to a more well-rounded set of concepts. Once sketches are complete, each participant creates a more detailed version of their favourite solution, including any features or steps that would make the idea work for users.

The sketch phase wraps up with each team member presenting their refined ideas in a "solution sketch," which includes annotations or simple diagrams to explain how the idea addresses the challenge. This presentation not only helps clarify each concept but also primes the team for the selection process on Day 3. By the end of the sketch phase, the team has a collection of possible solutions that will be evaluated and narrowed down in the next stage.

3. Decide (Day 3)

The decide phase is crucial for choosing the solution that the team will bring to life in the prototype. On this day, the team gathers to evaluate and discuss the sketches created in the previous phase. They carefully consider the feasibility, potential impact, and alignment with the problem statement for each solution. Voting methods like "heat mapping," where participants place dots on their favourite elements from each sketch, help streamline the decision-making process and objectively identify ideas that resonate with the group. This voting approach makes the selection process more democratic and reduces the influence of dominant voices.

After initial voting, the team conducts a group discussion to finalize the choice. They may weigh the strengths and weaknesses of each top solution, identifying any elements that could be combined to create an optimal prototype. The goal is to ensure that the chosen concept aligns with the challenge's objectives and will provide valuable insights during testing. At this stage, the team also considers any constraints or technical requirements that may impact the solution's feasibility. This process refines the solution even further, honing in on the most promising ideas that will be tested.

Once the team has decided on a direction, they create a storyboard to detail each step of the user journey with the solution. This storyboard serves as a blueprint for the prototype, mapping out interactions, key features, and the flow of the user experience. Storyboarding ensures everyone has a shared vision of how the prototype will function, which minimises misunderstandings and keeps the team aligned for the next phase. By the end of Day 3, the team has a focussed solution, and a clear plan is in place for building a prototype.

4. Prototype (Day 4)

On the fourth day, the team shifts to the hands-on task of building a prototype based on the storyboard. The aim here is not to create a perfect or fully functional product but rather to produce a simple, low-fidelity version that users can interact with. This quick-and-dirty approach allows the team to test the core functionality and design without investing too much time in details. Tools like clickable wireframes, basic mockups, and physical models are commonly used to create prototypes that provide a realistic sense of the solution's interaction flow.

The prototype phase emphasises collaboration, with each team member contributing according to their expertise—designers focus on layout and visuals, developers ensure the prototype functions as intended, and other team members handle content or scenarios for testing. The entire process is streamlined, and the team often breaks down tasks so that they can create the prototype within a single day. Building the prototype quickly encourages the team to prioritise essential features, focusing on what will provide the most meaningful feedback during testing.

By the end of this phase, the team has a tangible version of the solution that is ready to be tested with real users. This prototype will serve as the foundation for gathering insights on the final day of the sprint. A well-prepared prototype provides users with a realistic experience of the solution, which is essential for capturing accurate feedback and understanding how well it addresses their needs.

5. Test (Day 5)

The final day of the sprint is dedicated to testing the prototype with real users. This phase is where the team's work comes to life, as users interact with the solution and provide direct feedback on its usability and effectiveness. Typically, the team conducts one-on-one user interviews while observing users' interactions with the prototype. This allows them to identify pain points, moments of confusion, and areas where the solution resonates with users. The insights gained from user feedback are invaluable, as they reveal what works, what doesn't, and how the solution can be improved.

In addition to interviews, the team often uses observational techniques to gain deeper insights. Observing users in action allows the team to see unspoken reactions—such as hesitation, surprise, or frustration—that reveal underlying issues not always captured in verbal feedback. Testing also helps validate assumptions made during the sprint and determines whether the solution aligns with user needs. The feedback gathered on Day 5 gives the team a clear direction on the next steps, whether that involves refining the solution, developing it further, or even reconsidering the approach based on unexpected findings.

The sprint concludes with a debriefing session, where the team reviews all user feedback, identifies actionable insights, and decides on the way forward. This wrap-up discussion solidifies the lessons learned during the sprint and ensures alignment on the next steps. The test phase encapsulates the sprint's primary goal: to test ideas in a real-world context before committing to large-scale development, thereby minimizing risk and maximizing the chances of creating a solution that truly meets user needs.

Chapter 8: The Corporate Innovation Office, the Catalyst for Innovation

What Is a Corporate Innovation Office?

A corporate innovation office (CIO) is a dedicated entity within an organisation that actively manages the entire innovation process, from ideation to commercialisation. It plays a pivotal role in creating an environment where new ideas can flourish by providing the necessary frameworks, resources, and tools to support innovation at all levels of the organisation. This office often works with various internal departments such as R&D, marketing, and operations to identify synergies, reduce silos, and facilitate cross-functional collaboration, ensuring that innovation initiatives are seamlessly integrated into the company's operations and strategies.

In addition to fostering collaboration, a CIO also centralises and standardises innovation processes, making them more efficient and scalable. By implementing standardised methodologies like design thinking, agile project management, and lean startup principles, the CIO can accelerate the ideation and prototyping phases, reducing time-to-market for new products and services.

This structured approach helps the company maintain a balanced innovation portfolio, ranging from incremental improvements to breakthrough innovations, which is essential for sustained growth and long-term success.

Furthermore, the CIO acts as the organisation's innovation "nerve centre," serving as both a think tank and a testing ground for new ideas. It provides a space where cross-departmental teams can experiment without the fear of failure, supported by resources that would be challenging to secure in more traditional or siloed structures. This centralisation of innovation efforts also ensures that all projects align with the company's strategic goals, reducing redundancy and focusing resources on high-impact initiatives. By fostering a culture that encourages risk-taking and calculated experimentation, the CIO empowers employees to contribute ideas that drive meaningful change and long-term value creation.

Why Is a Corporate Innovation Office Important?

The importance of a corporate innovation office extends beyond simply keeping up with industry trends; it's a critical factor in sustaining a company's market relevance. In an era where technology, customer expectations, and competition evolve rapidly, the CIO acts as the company's internal engine for continuous improvement and adaptation. Through its coordinated approach to ideation, development, and commercialisation, the innovation office helps companies respond to disruptions and capitalise on new opportunities before competitors, thereby maintaining a strong market position and customer base.

Moreover, a CIO provides strategic foresight by identifying potential industry shifts and emerging technologies, enabling the organisation to respond proactively rather than reactively. This forward-looking approach allows companies to future-proof their offerings and maintain a competitive edge. By analysing market trends, studying competitor activities, and leveraging customer insights, the CIO ensures that innovation is not only about novelty but also aligns with real customer needs and demands. This strategic function of the CIO contributes to the organisation's resilience and adaptability, which are critical in navigating uncertain and fluctuating markets.

Another essential function of the CIO is cultivating a company-wide innovation culture that extends beyond the confines of the innovation office itself. By implementing programmes such as innovation workshops, hackathons, and idea incubators, the CIO helps foster an innovative mindset across departments, encouraging employees at all levels to think creatively and contribute to the company's growth. This focus on internal culture change helps break down silos and empowers employees to feel like stakeholders in the company's innovation journey, leading to greater engagement, collaboration, and ownership of new initiatives.

Organizational Designs for Innovation: The Structure of a Corporate Innovation Office

CENTRALIZED MODEL

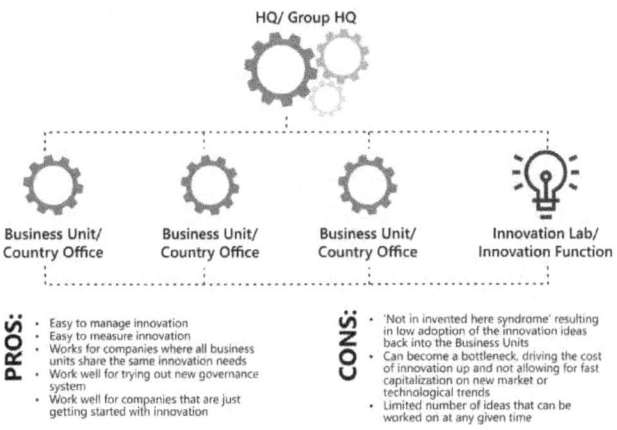

HQ/ Group HQ

Business Unit/ Country Office | Business Unit/ Country Office | Business Unit/ Country Office | Innovation Lab/ Innovation Function

PROS:
- Easy to manage innovation
- Easy to measure innovation
- Works for companies where all business units share the same innovation needs
- Work well for trying out new governance system
- Work well for companies that are just getting started with innovation

CONS:
- 'Not in invented here syndrome' resulting in low adoption of the innovation ideas back into the Business Units
- Can become a bottleneck, driving the cost of innovation up and not allowing for fast capitalization on new market or technological trends
- Limited number of ideas that can be worked on at any given time

Source: adjusted from weareoutcome.co

Centralised Innovation Structure

In a centralised innovation structure, all innovation activities are consolidated within a single department or office, often led by a chief innovation officer (CINO). This structure offers a high degree of control over the innovation process, enabling consistent standards, streamlined communication, and a unified approach to achieving the organisation's strategic goals. Centralised innovation is particularly effective in ensuring that all projects align closely with the organisation's overall vision and that resources are efficiently allocated. The centralised team is typically responsible for ideation, R&D, prototyping, and developing commercialisation strategies.

147

One of the primary benefits of a centralised structure is that it minimises redundancy and encourages a more organised allocation of resources. By centralising resources, the company can invest heavily in specialised innovation tools, methodologies, and talent, which may otherwise be challenging to maintain across various departments. This structure also provides clear accountability since a single department oversees innovation, allowing for more focussed performance measurement and objective-setting, which is essential for evaluating success.

Centralisation also enables a consistent innovation culture that reinforces core values, vision, and mission across all initiatives. The centralised team can standardise practices, ensuring that all projects are carried out with a shared philosophy, methodology, and set of expectations. This helps cultivate a cohesive innovation culture that is aligned with the company's brand and overarching strategy, making it easier for teams to adopt best practices, especially when collaborating on cross-functional projects.

However, the centralised innovation structure can face challenges with flexibility and responsiveness. With all activities directed through a single hub, the process of approving, developing, and implementing new ideas may become bottlenecked, leading to delays. Additionally, because innovation is centralised, there may be less opportunity for insights or initiatives originating from other departments, which could limit the diversity of ideas and reduce the company's agility in responding to unique departmental needs or market shifts.

Finally, for large organisations, centralisation may become unwieldy and lead to scalability issues. As the number of projects and the scale of innovation initiatives increase, a single department may struggle to effectively manage all activities. This limitation can cause slowdowns and hinder the company's ability to innovate at the speed necessary to maintain a competitive advantage. Thus, while centralised structures are ideal for aligning innovation with corporate goals, they may not be suitable for organisations requiring high agility and diverse ideation from all business units.

Decentralized Innovation Structure

DECENTRALIZED MODEL

HQ/ Group HQ

Business Unit/ Country Office

Business Unit/ Country Office

Business Unit/ Country Office

Innovation Lab/ Innovation Function

Innovation Lab/ Innovation Function

Innovation Lab/ Innovation Function

PROS:
- Allows for innovation at scale
- Easy to contextualize innovation to the needs of every Business Unit
- Each Business Unit can create and be responsible for their Innovation Strategy
- High rate of adoption of the validated ideas
- Ideal for companies with very distinct Business Unit for conglomerate companies

CONS:
- Difficult to align corporate strategy to Business Unit Innovation Strategy
- Susceptible for incosistencies and duplication
- Susceptible for insistence in governance
- Low cross-pollination
- Susceptible for multiple cultures evolving

Source: adjusted from weareoutcome.co

In a decentralised innovation structure, innovation is managed independently across various departments or business units within the organisation. Each unit is responsible for its own innovation activities, which allows teams to pursue initiatives that best align with their specific goals, customer needs, and industry trends. This structure supports flexibility and responsiveness, as decisions can be made at the department level without needing approval from a central office. Decentralisation is often preferred by companies with diverse product lines or markets that require unique approaches.

One of the greatest advantages of decentralised innovation is that it encourages a diverse range of ideas and solutions. With each business unit managing its own innovation, teams can tailor their approach based on direct insights from their market segments, allowing for faster adaptation and targeted solutions. This structure fosters creativity and supports the development of niche products, as innovation activities are tailored to the specific demands and opportunities of each unit's market.

Decentralisation also empowers employees and encourages a sense of ownership over innovation initiatives. When departments have autonomy over their projects, employees feel more connected to the outcome and motivated to drive meaningful change. This empowerment often leads to higher engagement and better results, as individuals are motivated to see their projects succeed within their specific business unit.

However, a decentralised structure can create challenges with alignment and resource allocation. Since each unit operates independently, it may be difficult to ensure that all innovation efforts align with the broader corporate strategy. This lack of alignment can result in duplicated efforts and inefficient use of resources. Additionally, without a central oversight function, it may be challenging to assess performance consistently across departments, making it harder to monitor ROI and measure success.

Finally, communication and knowledge sharing may be limited in a decentralised structure. When innovation is siloed across various units, it can be difficult to share insights, best practices, or valuable findings from one department to another. This isolation can lead to missed opportunities for cross-functional collaboration, which is often essential for tackling complex, cross-departmental challenges. As a result, decentralised innovation structures may require strong interdepartmental communication channels to facilitate effective knowledge sharing.

Hybrid Innovation Structure

HYBRID MODEL

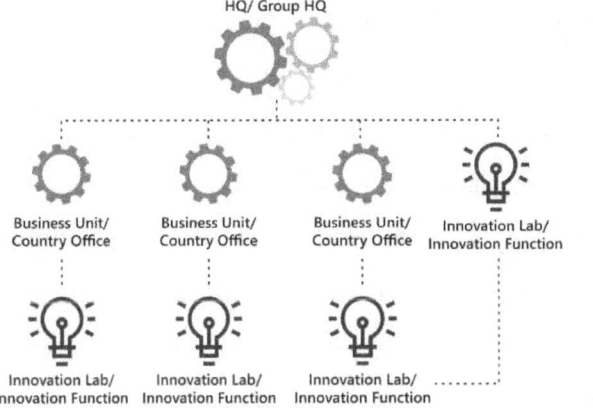

Source: adjusted from weareoutcome.co

A hybrid innovation structure combines elements of both centralised and decentralised approaches. In this structure, a central innovation team or office sets the overall strategy, standards, and resources, while individual departments or business units are empowered to execute innovation initiatives relevant to their specific goals. This balance allows for both alignment with corporate strategy and flexibility for units to pursue projects that meet their needs. Hybrid structures are increasingly popular as they offer the best of both worlds, leveraging centralized control with decentralised agility. Companies like Starbucks, ING, and Google are prime examples of organisations that successfully use this structure. Each has diverse product lines, services, and operational needs that require localised innovation, yet all maintain a core alignment with their central strategic vision, which keeps innovation efforts cohesive.

The hybrid model provides a clear framework for collaboration between the central innovation office and individual units. For instance, Starbucks centralises strategic innovation efforts to maintain brand consistency but allows regional teams the flexibility to adapt product offerings based on local preferences. This structure is highly advantageous in multinational settings or where divisions have differing needs but still require centralised coordination. Central teams at companies like ING set the innovation guidelines, while individual units create tailored solutions for regional market demands. This centralised support combined with decentralised action is key to adapting while maintaining brand integrity.

One of the main advantages of the hybrid structure is that it supports efficient resource management. Centralisation enables the company to make strategic investments in technology, tools, and training, which business units can leverage without needing to independently secure those resources. This shared pool of resources reduces duplication and maximizes efficiency while still providing business units with the autonomy to pursue initiatives that align with their unique objectives. Google, for example, benefits from a centralised research and development team, but individual divisions are given autonomy to drive innovation aligned with the company's core mission, enabling faster responses to specific market needs while utilising advanced central resources.

In addition, the hybrid model supports a culture of collaboration and cross-functional knowledge sharing. The central innovation office often facilitates interdepartmental collaboration by organising workshops, hackathons, and knowledge-sharing sessions where departments can exchange ideas and insights. For example, at Google, cross-departmental sharing is encouraged through various forums and events, fostering a continuous learning culture across the company. This collaborative environment not only enhances innovation outcomes but also builds a stronger organisational culture of continuous learning and improvement, ensuring the organisation remains competitive and agile.

Despite its strengths, a hybrid structure can be challenging to manage due to the need for clear governance and communication protocols. Striking the right balance between central oversight and departmental autonomy requires careful planning, as miscommunication or conflicting priorities between the central office and business units could hinder progress. Effective coordination and a shared vision are essential to maintaining alignment and maximising the effectiveness of the hybrid approach. The experiences of companies like Starbucks, ING, and Google demonstrate that the hybrid model is particularly suitable for large organisations with diverse needs across divisions, where central coordination can ensure consistency while still allowing for innovation flexibility across units.

The Responsibilities of the Corporate Innovation Office

The corporate innovation office in a hybrid innovation structure plays a critical role in aligning innovation efforts with the organisation's overall strategic objectives. Some of the key responsibilities of the corporate innovation office include:

Strategic Alignment and Vision Setting

One of the primary responsibilities of the corporate innovation office (CIO) is to establish a clear innovation strategy that aligns with the company's broader business objectives. This involves setting the vision and goals for innovation that support the organisation's mission, growth aspirations, and competitive positioning. By defining a clear vision, the CIO ensures that all innovation efforts contribute meaningfully to the company's strategic direction, providing a focus for the organisation's innovation activities. A well-aligned vision helps create a cohesive approach that integrates innovation into the core of the business rather than treating it as a separate, standalone activity.

To achieve this alignment, the CIO often conducts an analysis of market trends, emerging technologies, and customer needs to ensure that the innovation vision is both forward-looking and relevant. This requires close collaboration with other executive leaders to ensure that the innovation strategy supports and enhances other critical business functions. The CIO translates these findings into actionable objectives that guide the company's innovation roadmap, ensuring alignment with corporate priorities and long-term objectives.

Additionally, the CIO must communicate the innovation vision effectively across the organisation. By articulating the strategic importance of innovation, the CIO builds buy-in from all levels of the company and establishes a shared understanding of how innovation contributes to success. This alignment fosters a culture where employees across departments understand the role they play in achieving innovation goals, leading to greater engagement and cohesion.

The CIO also establishes key performance indicators (KPIs) to measure innovation success. These KPIs help the organisation track progress against the established vision and objectives, providing a framework to evaluate the impact of innovation initiatives on the company's strategic goals. By consistently monitoring and assessing these metrics, the CIO ensures that the innovation efforts are delivering value and can make adjustments if needed to keep projects aligned with business objectives.

Finally, the CIO is responsible for periodically reviewing and adjusting the innovation vision to adapt to changing market dynamics. Innovation is a continuous process that requires flexibility, and the CIO must be prepared to refine the strategy as new opportunities and challenges arise. By staying agile, the CIO ensures that the company remains competitive, relevant, and responsive to shifts in the business landscape, thereby enhancing the long-term viability of the organisation's innovation efforts.

Resource Allocation and Budgeting

Effective resource allocation and budgeting are crucial responsibilities of the corporate innovation office. Innovation initiatives often require significant investment in technology, talent, research, and development, and it's up to the CIO to ensure these resources are allocated efficiently. The CIO identifies which projects and departments require funding, balancing the need for high-potential, disruptive ideas with incremental improvements that deliver immediate value. By managing the innovation budget, the CIO can ensure that resources are distributed to maximise impact while controlling costs.

One of the key tasks in resource allocation is prioritising projects based on their strategic value and feasibility. The CIO evaluates each initiative's potential return on investment (ROI) and alignment with the organisation's goals, allocating resources to projects that offer the greatest potential for success. This prioritisation process often involves rigorous assessment, considering factors such as market potential, technological requirements, and operational demands. Effective prioritisation helps the organisation focus on high-impact projects and avoid wasting resources on initiatives with limited potential.

Beyond funding, resource allocation also involves securing and managing talent. Innovation requires diverse skill sets, and the CIO plays a key role in identifying, hiring, and developing employees with the expertise necessary to drive innovation. The CIO may collaborate with human resources to recruit specialists, form cross-functional teams, and ensure that team members have the skills and resources needed to execute their projects. By building strong innovation teams, the CIO supports a dynamic and capable workforce that can bring innovative ideas to fruition.

The CIO also oversees investment in technology and tools that support innovation. This can include research equipment, software, prototyping labs, and other infrastructure that enable employees to experiment and test new ideas. By providing access to advanced tools, the CIO empowers employees to explore creative solutions and facilitates a more efficient innovation process. Ensuring that all teams have the resources necessary to carry out their initiatives helps maintain momentum and encourages ongoing experimentation.

Lastly, the CIO is responsible for monitoring resource utilisation to ensure cost-effectiveness. This involves regularly reviewing project budgets, assessing spending patterns, and making adjustments where necessary. By keeping a close eye on expenses, the CIO can ensure that innovation projects remain financially viable and sustainable, which is critical for building long-term innovation capability within the organisation.

Innovation Culture Development

Fostering an innovation-friendly culture is a central responsibility of the CIO. The success of innovation initiatives largely depends on an organisational culture that encourages creativity, collaboration, and risk-taking. The CIO plays a key role in establishing and nurturing this culture, ensuring that employees feel empowered to contribute ideas and experiment with new approaches. By developing a culture that values innovation, the CIO creates an environment where employees feel motivated to participate actively in the innovation process.

One way the CIO promotes an innovation culture is by implementing programs that encourage idea generation and cross-functional collaboration. For example, the CIO may organise innovation workshops, hackathons, and brainstorming sessions where employees from different departments come together to share ideas and explore solutions. These activities foster an open, collaborative environment where employees feel comfortable proposing ideas and receiving feedback, which is essential for effective innovation.

In addition to fostering collaboration, the CIO encourages a mindset of calculated risk-taking. Innovation often involves exploring uncharted territory, and the CIO works to reduce the fear of failure by creating a supportive environment. This includes implementing policies that allow for experimentation and iteration without harsh penalties for unsuccessful outcomes. By promoting a "fail-fast, learn-fast" mentality, the CIO helps employees view failure as an opportunity to learn and improve rather than a setback.

The CIO also plays a role in recognising and rewarding innovative behaviour. By celebrating successful projects, highlighting creative contributions, and providing incentives for innovative ideas, the CIO reinforces the importance of innovation across the organisation. Recognising employees for their contributions not only boosts morale but also reinforces a culture where innovation is valued and rewarded.

Finally, the CIO continually reinforces the innovation culture by aligning it with the company's core values and mission. By embedding innovation into the company's identity, the CIO ensures that employees view innovation as an integral part of their roles rather than an additional responsibility. This cultural shift promotes sustained innovation efforts and empowers employees to think creatively in their daily work, contributing to a more dynamic, forward-thinking organisation.

Project Oversight and Management

Project oversight and management are crucial responsibilities for the CIO to ensure the success of innovation initiatives. The CIO oversees the end-to-end management of innovation projects, from ideation through development and commercialisation. This involves establishing project management frameworks and methodologies that provide structure and clarity for teams working on innovative solutions. By ensuring that projects are managed effectively, the CIO helps maintain momentum and supports a smooth transition from concept to execution.

An essential component of project management is setting milestones and tracking progress. The CIO defines key stages and performance indicators for each project, enabling teams to monitor their progress and identify potential issues early on. This milestone-driven approach helps teams stay focussed and ensures that projects are completed on time and within budget. By providing clear guidelines and regularly reviewing progress, the CIO supports accountability and keeps projects aligned with overall business goals.

The CIO also plays a role in managing risk and navigating potential challenges in innovation projects. Innovation often involves uncertainty, and the CIO is responsible for identifying and mitigating risks that could impact project success. This includes evaluating potential technological, financial, and operational risks and implementing strategies to address these challenges proactively. By managing risks effectively, the CIO helps ensure that innovation projects remain viable and resilient against obstacles.

In addition to overseeing individual projects, the CIO coordinates project prioritisation and portfolio management. With multiple innovation projects running simultaneously, the CIO must allocate resources and attention to high-priority initiatives while managing the overall project portfolio. This involves balancing short-term wins with long-term strategic projects, ensuring that the company's innovation pipeline is diverse and aligned with its business objectives.

Lastly, the CIO facilitates knowledge sharing and collaboration across projects. By encouraging teams to share insights, challenges, and successes, the CIO creates a learning environment where employees can benefit from each other's experiences. This knowledge-sharing culture supports continuous improvement, enhances team capabilities, and contributes to the success of future innovation projects, ultimately strengthening the organisation's overall innovation capabilities.

External Partnerships and Ecosystem Building

The corporate innovation office is also responsible for building and maintaining external partnerships to enhance the company's innovation capabilities. Today's innovation landscape often involves collaboration with external stakeholders, such as startups, universities, research institutions, and industry partners. The CIO is responsible for identifying and developing these relationships to access new knowledge, technologies, and market insights that complement the company's internal innovation efforts.

One way the CIO enhances the innovation ecosystem is by establishing partnerships with technology providers and startups. By collaborating with agile, innovative firms, the company gains access to cutting-edge solutions and can explore emerging technologies without investing in full-scale internal development. These partnerships enable the company to accelerate innovation and remain competitive in fast-paced markets where speed is essential.

In addition to partnerships with startups, the CIO also builds relationships with academic institutions and research organisations. Collaborating with universities and research centres allows the company to leverage advanced research capabilities and gain insights into new scientific discoveries. These partnerships often provide the company with early access to groundbreaking technologies and can serve as a pipeline for recruiting highly skilled talent.

The CIO also seeks industry partnerships and consortiums to participate in collaborative innovation efforts within the industry. By joining forces with other companies, the organisation can address shared challenges, influence industry standards, and gain a deeper understanding of market trends. These collaborations are especially valuable in industries where regulatory or technological challenges require collective problem-solving and innovation.

Lastly, the CIO is responsible for managing intellectual property (IP) and safeguarding innovations developed through partnerships. As the company collaborates with external partners, the CIO establishes guidelines for protecting proprietary information and managing IP rights. By developing clear agreements and maintaining strong governance over these collaborations, the CIO ensures that the organisation's innovations are protected and that partnerships generate mutually beneficial outcomes.

Role in Corporate Innovation Office

1. Executive Leadership

At the top of the corporate innovation office is the executive leadership, typically held by the chief innovation officer (CINO) or head of innovation. This leader is responsible for establishing the strategic vision and goals for innovation within the organization. The executive leader collaborates closely with other C-suite members to ensure the innovation strategy aligns with overall corporate objectives, growth targets, and competitive positioning. Through this alignment, the CINO sets the tone and priority for innovation across the company, ensuring that all efforts contribute directly to the organisation's core mission.

The CINO plays a key role in fostering a culture of innovation by championing new ideas and supporting creative thinking throughout the company. As the face of innovation efforts, they encourage employees to take part in innovation initiatives, fostering an inclusive environment where individuals feel empowered to contribute their ideas. This leadership position is instrumental in promoting a "fail-fast" mindset, where experimentation and learning from setbacks are encouraged as part of the innovation process.

In addition to setting the vision, the CINO is responsible for securing resources and support for innovation projects. They work closely with finance and executive teams to secure budget allocations and advocate for the resources necessary to execute innovation initiatives. By securing resources, the CINO ensures that teams have the tools, technology, and funding needed to bring ideas from concept to execution, driving innovation effectively within the organisation.

The executive leader also has a role in establishing metrics and KPIs for innovation success. They set measurable goals for innovation outcomes and track progress over time, enabling the organisation to assess the impact of innovation initiatives. By monitoring these metrics, the CINO can make informed decisions about which projects to continue, pivot, or scale, creating a data-driven approach to innovation management.

Lastly, the CINO is responsible for external representation and partnerships. They may engage with other organisations, academic institutions, or government bodies to form strategic alliances and partnerships that complement the company's internal innovation efforts. By expanding the organisation's innovation ecosystem through external collaboration, the CINO enables the company to tap into broader resources, market insights, and technology trends, enhancing its overall innovation capacity.

2. Innovation Strategy Team

The innovation strategy team is responsible for developing and aligning the innovation strategy with corporate objectives. This team works under the direction of the CINO to translate high-level innovation goals into actionable plans that align with the organisation's long-term vision. Their primary task is to identify priority areas for innovation, which could include emerging technologies, new market opportunities, or operational efficiencies. By defining these focus areas, the strategy team provides a clear direction for innovation efforts across the organisation.

To create an effective strategy, the team conducts extensive market research, analysing trends, competitive movements, and customer needs. This research provides valuable insights into where innovation efforts should be focussed and highlights opportunities for differentiation and competitive advantage. Additionally, the team assesses internal capabilities and resources to ensure that the innovation strategy is both ambitious and achievable within the company's current framework.

The innovation strategy team also collaborates with various business units and departments to ensure that innovation goals are well integrated into the broader corporate strategy. By engaging stakeholders across the organisation, they create alignment and buy-in, ensuring that innovation is not viewed as a siloed function but as an integral part of each department's objectives. This collaboration helps bridge the gap between strategic vision and operational execution.

Once the strategy is set, the team is responsible for defining the innovation roadmap. This roadmap outlines key initiatives, timelines, and milestones for the company's innovation journey, providing a clear plan for implementation. The roadmap serves as a guide for other parts of the CIO, ensuring that all teams are working toward common goals and that projects are launched in a coordinated, efficient manner.

Finally, the innovation strategy team monitors and evaluates the progress of innovation initiatives against the roadmap and KPIs. They collect feedback, conduct regular assessments, and adjust the strategy as needed to respond to changes in the market or internal priorities. This adaptive approach allows the company to remain agile and responsive, ensuring that the innovation strategy remains relevant and effective.

3. Innovation Labs

Innovation labs are specialized teams or dedicated spaces within the CIO where experimentation, prototyping, and testing of new ideas occur. These labs provide an environment for cross-functional collaboration, allowing employees from different backgrounds to work together on creative solutions. With access to advanced tools and technologies, innovation labs serve as a playground for ideation, where ideas can be explored and developed into viable concepts without the constraints of everyday business operations.

The labs are often structured to encourage rapid prototyping and iterative development, allowing teams to quickly test and refine ideas. By employing agile methodologies, innovation labs enable teams to experiment with new solutions, gather feedback, and make improvements in a continuous loop. This iterative approach reduces the time to market for new ideas and allows for quick pivots in response to challenges or insights gained during testing.

In addition to providing a testing ground for new ideas, innovation labs support a culture of risk-taking. Employees are encouraged to experiment without the fear of failure, as the lab environment is designed to promote learning and adaptation. The emphasis on "learning by doing" encourages a mindset where failure is seen as an opportunity for growth, contributing to a more resilient and innovative organisational culture.

The innovation labs also serve as a bridge between internal and external innovation. By inviting partners, customers, or industry experts into the lab environment, the CIO fosters open innovation, where diverse perspectives can enrich the development process. These collaborations can bring in fresh insights, helping the organisation stay ahead of industry trends and incorporate best practices from other sectors.

Finally, innovation labs provide tangible proof of the organisation's commitment to innovation. The existence of a physical or virtual lab space demonstrates that the company is serious about investing in creative solutions and supporting forward-thinking employees. By maintaining a visible lab environment, the CIO reinforces the importance of innovation as a core part of the organisation's identity and values.

4. Corporate Venture Capital (CVC)

The corporate venture capital (CVC) function within the CIO manages investments in startups and strategic acquisitions that complement the company's internal innovation efforts. The CVC team identifies promising external companies that align with the organisation's innovation goals, providing funding, mentorship, and strategic guidance. These investments allow the organisation to access cutting-edge technologies and business models that may be challenging or time-intensive to develop internally.

One key responsibility of the CVC team is to conduct thorough due diligence on potential investment opportunities. This process involves evaluating the startup's technology, market potential, financial stability, and alignment with the organisation's goals. By carefully selecting investments, the CVC team minimizes risk and ensures that each partnership adds tangible value to the organisation's innovation portfolio.

The CVC team also plays an active role in fostering collaboration between the startup and the company. They facilitate integration efforts, where applicable, ensuring that the startup's capabilities and solutions can be seamlessly incorporated into the organisation's operations. This integration allows the company to leverage the startup's innovations quickly and effectively, enhancing its competitive advantage and expanding its product or service offerings.

Beyond financial investment, the CVC team often provides mentorship and resources to the startups they invest in. This support includes access to industry experts, market insights, and technology resources, enabling the startup to scale and succeed. By creating a supportive ecosystem for their portfolio companies, the CVC team ensures that the partnership benefits both parties and maximizes the impact of the investment.

Finally, the CVC function helps the organisation stay informed about emerging trends and disruptive innovations in the market. By actively engaging with startups and monitoring the venture capital landscape, the CVC team provides valuable insights into new developments that could shape the future of the industry. This foresight enables the organisation to adapt quickly to market changes and positions it as a proactive, forward-thinking industry leader.

5. Support Functions

The support functions within the CIO provide essential services that enable innovation projects to operate smoothly and remain compliant with corporate policies and industry regulations. These functions include legal, finance, human resources, and communications teams, each playing a specific role in supporting the broader innovation mission. By handling administrative and regulatory tasks, support functions allow innovation teams to focus on creative work without getting bogged down by operational details.

The legal team, for example, ensures that all innovation initiatives comply with relevant laws and regulations. This includes protecting intellectual property (IP), managing patents, and ensuring that new products or solutions meet industry standards. The legal team also drafts agreements and handles IP rights in partnerships, safeguarding the organisation's interests and minimising risk in collaborative ventures.

The finance team manages budgets, funding allocations, and financial reporting for innovation projects. They work closely with the CINO to allocate resources strategically, ensuring that projects are adequately funded and financially viable. The finance team also monitors expenses and ROI, providing transparency and accountability for innovation spending, which is crucial for maintaining executive and stakeholder support.

Human resources (HR) plays a critical role in recruiting and developing talent for innovation teams. HR collaborates with the CIO to identify skill gaps, hire new employees with specialised expertise, and facilitate training and development programs. By building a strong talent pipeline, HR ensures that the organisation has the skills and knowledge needed to drive continuous innovation.

The communications team is responsible for promoting the organisation's innovation efforts both internally and externally. They share success stories, highlight key projects, and communicate the organisation's commitment to innovation. Effective communication helps build morale among employees, attracts potential partners, and reinforces the company's brand as an innovative leader in the industry.

Finally, support functions help create a cohesive innovation ecosystem by ensuring that all initiatives are aligned with corporate policies and culture. By integrating legal, financial, HR, and communication support, the CIO can manage innovation projects more effectively and ensure that these initiatives contribute to the organisation's strategic goals. This coordinated support enables the CIO to focus on driving impactful innovation within a structured, compliant, and well-resourced environment.

Appendix

Corporate Innovation Maturity Assessment

The **Corporate Innovation Maturity Assessment** developed by the **Board of Transformation and Excellence (BTX)** is a comprehensive tool designed to evaluate an organisation's readiness and capability to drive innovation across all levels. This assessment helps organisations measure how well they embrace innovation, adapt to market changes, and deliver value to their customers through transformative ideas and processes. The framework consists of multiple dimensions, each of which addresses a critical area of innovation within the organisation, ranging from leadership commitment to the effectiveness of tools and technologies.

The goal of this assessment is to provide actionable insights into an organisation's innovation maturity by analysing key areas such as business impact, team dynamics, leadership, process effectiveness, and technological adoption. By identifying strengths and opportunities for improvement, organisations can establish a clear roadmap for accelerating innovation, optimising resources, and fostering a culture that thrives on creativity and agility.

How to Use the Corporate Innovation Maturity Assessment

1. **Self-Assessment or External Review**: Organisations can use this assessment either as a self-assessment tool or

engage with BTX experts to perform a detailed evaluation. The self-assessment approach allows organisations to assess their current state of innovation independently, while an external review by BTX experts can provide an unbiased perspective on the organisation's innovation maturity.

2. **Identify Strengths and Gaps**: The assessment is organized into **10 key dimensions**, each with multiple sub-dimensions. Each dimension is assessed using statements that help organisations gauge their maturity level. By evaluating these statements, organisations can identify their strengths as well as areas that need improvement.

3. **Score and Measure Progress**: Each statement is rated on a scale 1 to 10 (e.g., from Low = "Not at all" to High "Fully met"), providing organisations with a maturity score. This score can be used to track progress over time, allowing organisations to benchmark themselves against industry standards or their own innovation goals.

4. **Actionable Insights**: Based on the results of the assessment, organisations can receive recommendations and insights into specific actions they can take to improve their innovation maturity. These actions may include developing leadership capabilities, enhancing cross-functional collaboration, adopting emerging technologies, or refining their innovation processes.

5. **Continuous Improvement**: The Corporate Innovation Maturity Assessment is not a one-time exercise; it is meant to be used periodically to monitor progress and refine innovation strategies. By continuously assessing innovation maturity, organisations can adapt to market changes, optimise their innovation efforts, and stay competitive in an increasingly dynamic environment.

Key Dimensions in the Assessment

The Corporate Innovation Maturity Assessment by BTX covers the following dimensions:

1. **Business & Customer Impact**: Measures how well innovations create value for customers and drive business outcomes.

2. **People**: Assesses how well the organisation fosters creativity, collaboration, and skill development within its teams.

3. **Leadership**: Evaluates the ability of leadership to drive and sustain innovation across the organisation.

4. **Structure**: Focuses on how well organisational structures and processes support innovation efforts.

5. **Process**: Assesses the effectiveness of innovation processes, from idea generation to execution.

6. **Tools & Technology**: Evaluates how well tools and technologies support the innovation process, including collaboration, monitoring, and scalability.

7. **Culture of Innovation**: Assesses the organisational culture's support for innovation, risk-taking, and learning from failure.

8. **Innovation Strategy & Vision**: Measures how well innovation strategies align with the overall business vision and objectives.

9. **Idea Management**: Focuses on how well the organisation generates, evaluates, and scales new ideas.

10. **Risk Management & Compliance**: Evaluates how well risks are managed in the innovation process and ensures compliance with relevant regulations.

By following this structured assessment, organisations can gain clarity on where they stand in their innovation journey and create a tailored plan to drive further innovation and growth. The Corporate Innovation Maturity Assessment by BTX serves as a powerful tool for organisations aiming to stay ahead in an era where innovation is crucial for success.

Ready to take the next step in enhancing your organisation's innovation maturity? As you embark on your journey to greater innovation, use the insights provided by the Corporate Innovation Maturity Assessment to guide your strategy and growth. To get started, contact us at hello@boardoftransformation.com. Our team at BTX is here to help you unlock your organisation's full potential and transform your innovation practices into a competitive advantage!

Dimension: Business and Customer Impact

Sub-dimension	Description	Statement	Rate 1-10 (Low– High)
Innovation-Driven Customer Impact	Focuses on how well innovations create value for customers and solve evolving needs.	➢ Our innovations consistently address customers' most critical needs and pain points. ➢ We focus on creating solutions that deliver measurable improvements in customer outcomes. ➢ Our new products and services are designed to anticipate future customer demands. ➢ We prioritise innovations that enable customers to achieve their goals more efficiently. ➢ Our organisation measures the success of innovations based on the value they create for customers.	
		Average Score	
Customer Feedback	Measures how effectively customer feedback is incorporated into the innovation process.	➢ We actively gather customer feedback at every stage of the innovation lifecycle. ➢ Customer feedback directly influences the design and improvement of our solutions. ➢ We have a structured process to collect, analyse, and act on customer feedback promptly. ➢ Our teams use customer feedback to prioritise features and enhancements in our products. ➢ Customer suggestions and complaints are regularly reviewed and implemented to refine innovations.	
		Average Score	
Market Responsiveness	Assesses how quickly and effectively the organisation adapts to market demands and changes.	➢ We monitor market trends to quickly identify emerging opportunities and threats. ➢ Our organisation adapts its products and services to meet shifting market expectations. ➢ We have a framework to rapidly test and implement changes in response to market dynamics. ➢ Our teams regularly review competitor activities to ensure our	

		offerings remain competitive. ➤ We excel at launching innovations that address urgent and time-sensitive customer needs.	
		Average Score	
Customer Satisfaction Metrics	Evaluates the use of data and metrics to measure and enhance customer satisfaction from innovations.	➤ We consistently track customer satisfaction using tools like Net Promoter Score (NPS) and feedback surveys. ➤ Customer satisfaction metrics are integrated into the evaluation of our innovation projects. ➤ We use data to identify gaps in satisfaction and address them through targeted improvements. ➤ Our organisation benchmarks customer satisfaction levels against industry standards. ➤ We leverage real-time analytics to monitor customer satisfaction trends and respond proactively.	
		Average Score	
		Total Score	

Dimension: Innovation Strategy & Vision

Sub-dimension	Description	Statement	Rate 1-10 (Low – High)
Strategic Alignment	Measures how well innovation aligns with the overall organisational strategy.	➤ Innovation goals are aligned with the company's overall strategic objectives. ➤ Leadership ensures that innovation initiatives reflect the company's long-term vision. ➤ Teams are consistently reminded of the strategic purpose behind innovation efforts. ➤ Innovation strategies are communicated clearly to all departments to align efforts. ➤ Projects are evaluated based on how well they support the company's core objectives.	
		Average Score	
Long-Term Innovation Focus	Assesses the commitment to innovation as a sustained, strategic priority.	➤ The organisation prioritises long-term innovation goals over short-term gains. ➤ Innovation is seen as a key driver for the company's future growth and sustainability. ➤ Resources are allocated to innovation initiatives with long-term value. ➤ Leadership consistently champions the importance of long-term innovation. ➤ Innovation planning includes clear long-term objectives with measurable outcomes.	
		Average Score	
Innovation Portfolio Management	Evaluates how projects are balanced in terms of risk, resources, and value.	➤ Innovation projects are balanced across different levels of risk and return. ➤ A structured portfolio management process ensures the right mix of innovation projects. ➤ Resources are allocated efficiently based on the potential impact of each innovation. ➤ Regular reviews are held to assess	

		the progress and viability of the innovation portfolio.	
		➢ Innovation projects are adjusted as necessary to align with changing business needs.	
		Average Score	
Innovation Prioritization	Focuses on how well initiatives are prioritised based on strategic impact.	➢ The organisation effectively prioritises projects that align with customer needs and business objectives. ➢ Prioritisation is driven by data and the expected return on innovation investments. ➢ Teams are clear on which innovation initiatives are the most critical to pursue. ➢ The prioritisation process includes input from all relevant stakeholders. ➢ The innovation strategy continuously adapts based on changing market conditions and customer feedback.	
		Average Score	
		Total Score	

Dimension: People

Sub-dimension	Description	Statement	Rate 1-10 (Low – High)
Creativity & Collaboration	Fosters creative thinking and collaboration among team members to drive innovation.	➤ Team members actively brainstorm and collaborate to solve complex challenges. ➤ Cross-functional teams are encouraged to share diverse perspectives during innovation discussions. ➤ Collaboration tools and practices help streamline communication and creativity within teams. ➤ The organisation provides workshops to enhance creative problem-solving skills. ➤ Team creativity is celebrated through the recognition of innovative ideas.	
		Average Score	
Skill Development	Assesses the opportunities and investment in training to build innovation capabilities.	➤ Employees receive regular training to stay updated on the latest innovation trends. ➤ Leadership invests in mentorship programs to develop innovation skills. ➤ Learning resources are easily accessible to all employees. ➤ Teams are encouraged to attend external conferences and events to expand their expertise. ➤ Personal growth plans include goals related to innovation capability building.	
		Average Score	
Autonomy & Empowerment	Measures the level of decision-making power given to teams in the innovation process.	➤ Teams have the freedom to make decisions critical to their projects. ➤ Employees are encouraged to take ownership of their innovative ideas. ➤ Leaders trust teams to manage projects without micromanagement. ➤ Autonomy is promoted by allowing flexible approaches to problem-solving. ➤ Team members are empowered to	

		challenge the status quo to achieve better results.	
		Average Score	
Psychological Safety	Evaluates how safe employees feel in sharing ideas and taking risks	➢ Employees feel confident sharing unconventional ideas without fear of judgment. ➢ Leaders provide constructive feedback to encourage open dialogue. ➢ Mistakes are treated as learning opportunities, not failures. ➢ Teams foster a culture of mutual respect and trust. ➢ Employees feel supported when proposing innovative but risky ideas.	
		Average Score	
		Total Score	

Dimension: Culture of Innovation

Sub-dimension	Description	Statement	Rate 1-10 (Low – High)
Innovation Mindset	Assesses how well the organisation promotes a culture of risk-taking and learning from failure.	➢ Employees are encouraged to view challenges as opportunities for innovation. ➢ Failure is seen as a necessary step in the learning process, fostering a growth mindset. ➢ The organisation celebrates creativity and supports individuals taking calculated risks. ➢ Innovation is deeply embedded in the culture and is reflected in everyday actions. ➢ Employees consistently think beyond the status quo and propose innovative solutions.	
		Average Score	
Collaboration and Knowledge Sharing	Focuses on fostering teamwork and knowledge exchange for innovation.	➢ Teams are incentivized to share ideas, knowledge, and resources across departments. ➢ Collaboration spaces, both physical and virtual, are available for spontaneous idea generation. ➢ Cross-functional collaboration is encouraged to tackle complex challenges with diverse perspectives. ➢ Knowledge-sharing platforms are actively used for continuous learning and innovation. ➢ The organisation values input from all levels and encourages an open exchange of ideas.	
		Average Score	

Recognition & Rewards	Evaluates how contributions to innovation are recognised and rewarded.	➤ Innovative contributions are publicly recognised during company-wide meetings. ➤ Employees who bring forth impactful ideas are rewarded with opportunities for career advancement. ➤ Teams are celebrated for successfully implementing creative solutions. ➤ Rewards for innovation are tied to both the impact and creativity of the solutions. ➤ Recognition programs are regularly updated to stay aligned with innovation goals.	
		Average Score	
Continuous Learning & Development	Encourages ongoing learning and experimentation to drive improvement.	➤ The organisation provides ongoing training and workshops to build innovation skills. ➤ Employees have access to resources that encourage experimentation and learning. ➤ Opportunities for mentorship are available to help individuals grow within their innovation roles. ➤ Regular knowledge-sharing sessions are organised to foster a culture of continuous learning. ➤ Development plans are designed to challenge employees and expand their innovation capabilities.	
		Average Score	
		Total Score	

Dimension: Leadership

Sub-dimension	Description	Statement	Rate 1-10 (Low – High)
Innovation Leadership & Vision	Focuses on how well leadership communicates the vision and strategic direction for innovation.	➤ Leaders articulate a clear vision for innovation that inspires teams. ➤ Strategic goals align with the organisation's innovation objectives. ➤ Leaders regularly communicate progress and updates on innovation initiatives. ➤ Leadership provides clarity on how innovation contributes to long-term goals. ➤ Teams understand the direction and purpose of ongoing innovation efforts.	
		Average Score	
Servant Leadership	Assesses how leaders support and empower teams to foster innovation.	➤ Leaders actively remove obstacles that hinder team innovation efforts. ➤ Managers prioritize the needs of their teams over their own. ➤ Leadership promotes an inclusive environment where every voice is valued. ➤ Resources and support are made readily available to enable innovation. ➤ Leaders encourage team collaboration and personal development.	
		Average Score	
Change Advocacy	Evaluates leadership's ability to drive and support transformational initiatives.	➤ Leadership embraces change and inspires others to adapt to new strategies. ➤ Leaders take ownership of driving organisational transformation. ➤ Teams receive clear guidance and support during periods of change. ➤ Innovation initiatives are backed by leadership at every level. ➤ Leaders champion experimentation and challenge traditional norms.	

		Average Score	
Decision-Making Agility	Measures the speed and flexibility of leadership in making innovation-related decisions.	➤ Leadership embraces change and inspires others to adapt to new strategies. ➤ Leaders take ownership of driving organisational transformation. ➤ Teams receive clear guidance and support during periods of change. ➤ Innovation initiatives are backed by leadership at every level. ➤ Leaders champion experimentation and challenge traditional norms.	
		Average Score	
		Total Score	

Dimension: Structure

Sub-dimension	Description	Statement	Rate 1-10 (Low – High)
Cross-Functional Teams	Evaluates the effectiveness of diverse teams in driving innovation.	➢ Teams are formed with diverse skills to ensure innovative outcomes. ➢ Collaboration across departments is prioritised to break down silos. ➢ Project teams are structured to include all necessary expertise. ➢ Cross-functional team achievements are celebrated to promote collaboration. ➢ Teams are given resources to work seamlessly on innovation initiatives.	
		Average Score	
Hierarchy Flexibility	Assesses how adaptable the organisational structure is to support innovation.	➢ Decision-making authority is decentralised to promote team autonomy. ➢ Layers of bureaucracy are minimised to support faster innovation processes. ➢ Leadership is accessible to employees at all levels for input and feedback. ➢ Hierarchical boundaries do not hinder collaboration or idea sharing. ➢ Teams are empowered to challenge traditional structures when necessary.	
		Average Score	
Role Clarity:	Measures the clarity of roles in supporting efficient collaboration.	➢ Every team member understands their role in the innovation process. ➢ Roles are designed to maximise collaboration and efficiency. ➢ Clear expectations are set for team contributions to innovation. ➢ Role alignment minimises overlap and confusion during project execution. ➢ Responsibilities are clearly communicated during team onboarding.	
		Average Score	

Resource Allocation	Examines how effectively resources are allocated to innovation projects.	➤ Innovation projects are prioritised during budget planning. ➤ Teams receive adequate resources to execute innovation initiatives effectively. ➤ Investments in innovation tools and technology are regularly reviewed. ➤ Resource allocation aligns with the strategic importance of innovation goals. ➤ Innovation initiatives are not delayed due to resource constraints.	
		Average Score	
		Total Score	

Dimension: Process

Sub-dimension	Description	Statement	Rate 1-10 (Low – High)
Innovation Lifecycle	Assesses the effectiveness of processes managing ideas from concept to execution.	➢ The organisation has a structured approach to managing the innovation lifecycle. ➢ Clear milestones are set for every stage of the innovation process. ➢ Teams follow a consistent process from ideation to execution. ➢ Innovation lifecycle processes are regularly reviewed and improved. ➢ Stakeholders are informed about each stage of the innovation journey.	
		Average Score	
Deliverable Predictability	Measures the consistency in completing innovation deliverables on time.	➢ Teams consistently deliver innovation outcomes within planned timelines. ➢ Iteration goals are met without compromising quality. ➢ Processes are streamlined to minimise disruptions in deliverables. ➢ Predictability is tracked using data from previous projects. ➢ Deliverables are aligned with expectations set during planning phases.	
		Average Score	
Feedback Loops	Evaluates how teams integrate feedback to improve innovation outcomes.	➢ Customer feedback is incorporated to refine innovation projects. ➢ Teams hold regular reviews to assess process effectiveness. ➢ Feedback is acted upon promptly to improve outcomes. ➢ Internal and external stakeholders provide iterative inputs. ➢ Feedback is tracked to ensure alignment with user needs.	
		Average Score	

188

Experimentation & Adaptability	Focuses on the ability to experiment and adapt based on results.	➤ Teams are encouraged to test innovative ideas with minimal constraints. ➤ Experimentation is supported by dedicated resources and tools. ➤ Hypotheses are validated before scaling innovation solutions. ➤ Processes are adapted based on the results of experiments. ➤ Experimentation outcomes inform future strategies.	
		Average Score	
		Total Score	

Dimension: Idea Management

Sub-dimension	Description	Statement	Rate 1-10 (Low – High)
Idea Generation	Focuses on processes and platforms to generate new ideas.	➤ The organisation encourages employees to contribute ideas to drive innovation. ➤ Idea generation is supported by platforms that make it easy for employees to submit concepts. ➤ Cross-functional brainstorming sessions are regularly organised to spark creativity. ➤ Innovation contests are held to motivate employees to propose new ideas. ➤ Idea-generation tools are widely used to collect and track creative solutions.	
		Average Score	
Idea Evaluation & Prioritization	Measures how ideas are assessed and prioritised for execution.	➤ Ideas are evaluated based on their feasibility, impact, and alignment with strategic goals. ➤ A formalized process ensures that only high-potential ideas move forward. ➤ Stakeholders are involved in the evaluation process to ensure diverse perspectives are considered. ➤ The prioritisation process considers both short-term and long-term innovation goals. ➤ Teams regularly review and refine the ideas in the pipeline to keep them relevant.	
		Average Score	
Prototyping & Experimentation	Assesses the speed and efficiency of turning ideas into prototypes.	➤ Prototyping tools are available to quickly bring ideas to life and test them. ➤ Teams are encouraged to experiment with low-cost prototypes to validate concepts. ➤ Rapid prototyping is seen as a key method for mitigating risk and refining ideas. ➤ Feedback loops are integrated into	

190

		prototyping to improve designs continuously.	
		➢ The organisation supports experimentation by providing necessary resources and space.	
		Average Score	
Idea Execution & Scaling	Evaluates processes for scaling successful ideas into impactful solutions.	➢ Successful ideas are rapidly scaled with proper resource allocation.	
		➢ The organisation has clear processes for turning ideas into implemented solutions.	
		➢ Teams are given the autonomy to scale innovative solutions that show potential.	
		➢ The execution process ensures alignment with business objectives and customer needs.	
		➢ The organisation ensures that scaling innovations doesn't sacrifice quality or customer experience.	
		Average Score	
		Total Score	

Dimension: Tools & Technology

Sub-dimension	Description	Statement	Rate 1-10 (Low – High)
Seamless & Real-Time Collaboration	Measures how tools support cross-location and real-time teamwork.	➤ Collaboration tools enable real-time communication across geographies. ➤ Teams can share updates instantly using integrated platforms. ➤ Collaboration platforms are intuitive and easy to use. ➤ Real-time brainstorming sessions are conducted using innovative tools. ➤ Cross-location collaboration is seamless, improving productivity.	
		Average Score	
Scalability & Flexibility	Evaluates technology's ability to scale innovation efforts.	➤ The technology stack is designed to handle an increasing volume of users or data as the business grows. ➤ Tools can easily adapt to accommodate expanding project requirements or new business needs without major reconfiguration. ➤ The infrastructure supports seamless scaling, allowing teams to innovate at a larger scale with minimal disruption. ➤ The technology is capable of supporting cross-team collaboration and scaling across multiple business units. ➤ As innovation efforts expand, the technology infrastructure automatically adjusts to ensure continued efficiency and performance.	
		Average Score	
Security & Compliance	Ensures that tools adhere to data security and regulatory standards.	➤ The tools in use are compliant with industry-specific data protection laws and regulations, ensuring secure handling of customer data. ➤ Regular security audits are conducted to assess and ensure compliance with current security standards. ➤ All tools used in innovation	

		processes implement encryption and data protection measures to safeguard sensitive information.	
		➤ Tools are updated regularly to reflect the latest security patches and to maintain compliance with changing regulations.	
		➤ The organisation's use of technology aligns with global data protection standards, ensuring customer privacy and trust.	
		Average Score	
Emerging Technology	Assesses the organisation's use of new and innovative technologies to drive innovation	➤ The organisation actively explores and integrates emerging technologies such as AI, blockchain, and IoT to enhance innovation.	
		➤ Teams leverage cutting-edge tools and platforms to improve efficiency and create new value propositions for customers.	
		➤ The use of emerging technologies enables the organisation to stay ahead of market trends and disrupt traditional business models.	
		➤ New technology solutions are rapidly evaluated and implemented to test their potential for driving business transformation.	
		➤ The organisation is open to experimenting with unconventional, emerging tech to solve complex problems and meet evolving market demands.	
		Average Score	
		Total Score	

Dimension: Risk Management & Compliance

Sub-dimension	Description	Statement	Rate 1-10 (Low – High)
Innovation Risk Assessment	Measures how well risks are identified and managed in innovation projects.	➤ Risk assessments are regularly conducted to identify and mitigate innovation-related risks. ➤ Innovation risks are evaluated based on their potential impact on the business. ➤ A clear framework is in place to manage and reduce risks during the innovation process. ➤ Teams are trained to assess and address risks early in the innovation lifecycle. ➤ Leadership ensures that risk management is integrated into all stages of the innovation process.	
		Average Score	
Compliance with Regulations	Evaluates adherence to legal and regulatory standards during innovation efforts.	➤ The organisation adheres to all relevant laws and regulations while innovating. ➤ Compliance requirements are integrated into the innovation strategy from the outset. ➤ Legal and regulatory teams are involved early to ensure compliance throughout the innovation process. ➤ Teams are regularly trained on the legal aspects related to innovation and compliance. ➤ The organisation proactively monitors changes in regulations to ensure continuous compliance.	
		Average Score	
Risk-Taking Culture	Focuses on the organisation's willingness to embrace calculated risks for innovation.	➤ The organisation encourages calculated risks in pursuit of breakthrough innovations. ➤ Leaders create a safe environment for teams to experiment and learn from their failures. ➤ Risk-taking is balanced with a clear understanding of potential rewards.	

194

		➤ Employees are rewarded for successfully navigating risks that lead to valuable innovations. ➤ The organisation embraces a mindset that sees risks as opportunities for growth.	
		Average Score	
Contingency Planning & Mitigation	Assesses the ability to prepare for and mitigate potential innovation failures.	➤ Contingency plans are in place to address potential failures or unforeseen challenges in innovation initiatives. ➤ The organisation regularly updates risk mitigation strategies to stay ahead of potential issues. ➤ Teams are trained in crisis management to handle unexpected obstacles during innovation efforts. ➤ Resources are allocated to support rapid recovery from innovation setbacks. ➤ The organisation develops multiple solutions for high-risk innovation projects to ensure success.	
		Average Score	
		Total Score	

References

A Chief Innovation Officer's Actual Responsibilities. (2023, February 7).

hbr.org/2014/11/a-chief-innovation-officers-actual-responsibilities

Abreu, A. (2021) "Innovation Ecosystems: A Sustainability Perspective," Multidisciplinary Digital Publishing Institute, 13(4), p. 1675-1675. Available at:

https://doi.org/10.3390/su13041675.

Ahmed, K, P. (1999) "Sustaining a culture of discontinuous innovation," Elsevier BV, p. 374-405. Available at:

https://doi.org/10.1016/b978-0-7506-3953-8.50015-5.

Ahmed, P K. (1999, January 1). Sustaining a culture of discontinuous innovation. Elsevier BV, 374-405.

https://doi.org/10.1016/b978-0-7506-3953-8.50015-5

Al-Refaie, A., Rawabdeh, A, I. and AlKesbeh, A. (2014) "Factors Affecting Innovation in Jordanian Public Firms," IGI Global, 5(4), p. 73-87. Available at: https://doi.org/10.4018/ijissc.2014100105.

Alexander, A. et al. (2018) "Scanning the Future of Medical Imaging," Elsevier BV, 16(4), p. 501-507. Available at:

https://doi.org/10.1016/j.jacr.2018.09.050.

Allayannis, G. (2017, January 20). New Leaders of Financial Giants: The Cases of Vikram Pandit (Citi) and John Thain (Merrill

Lynch). Emerald Publishing Limited, 1-10.

https://doi.org/10.1108/case.darden.2016.000214

Amar, D, A. and Juneja, J. (2008) "A descriptive model of innovation and creativity in organizations: a synthesis of research and practice," Taylor & Francis, 6(4), p. 298-311. Available at: https://doi.org/10.1057/kmrp.2008.18.

Amazon Enters the Cloud Computing Business (no date). Available at:

https://web.stanford.edu/class/ee204/Publications/Amazon-EE353-2008-1.pdf.

Amazon's profitability (2023). Available at:

http://faculty.london.edu/chigson/casestudies/pdfs/Amazon.pdf.

Amazon.com (D) - Case (2024). Available at:

https://www.hbs.edu/faculty/Pages/item.aspx?num=28010.

Anand, N., & Daft, R L. (2007, January 1). What is the Right Organization Design? Elsevier BV, 36(4), 329-344.

https://doi.org/10.1016/j.orgdyn.2007.06.001

Anderson, J. and Markides, C. (2004) "t-INNOVATION: USING INFORMATION AND COMMUNICATION TECHNOLOGY TO ACHIEVE STRATEGIC INNOVATION," World Scientific, 01(02), p. 233-248. Available at:

https://doi.org/10.1142/s0219877004000179.

Apple announces ultra-thin laptop (2008). Available at:

http://news.bbc.co.uk/2/hi/technology/7188849.stm.

Barbieri, C, J. and Álvares, T, C, A. (2016) "Sixth generation innovation model: description of a success model," University of São Paulo, 13(2), p. 116-127. Available at:

https://doi.org/10.1016/j.rai.2016.04.004.

Barton, S. (2019, October 15). Azure Cosmos DB Technical Overview.

azure.microsoft.com/mediahandler/files/resourcefiles/five-steps-to-culture-change

Bate, J D., & Johnston, R E. (2005, February 1). Strategic frontiers: the starting-point for innovative growth. Emerald Publishing Limited, 33(1), 12-18.

https://doi.org/10.1108/10878570510572608

Belz, A P. (2010, March 1). Challenges in technology infusion: Adapting best practices from the private sector. , 1-7.

https://doi.org/10.1109/aero.2010.5446754

Board of Innovation (2024) What is innovation Strategy? Discover best practices, definitions, tools, and examples. Available at: https://www.boardofinnovation.com/what-is-innovation-strategy-discover-best-practices-definitions-tools-and-examples/ (Accessed: November 11, 2024).

Bowonder, B. et al. (2010) "Innovation Strategies for Creating Competitive Advantage," Taylor & Francis, 53(3), p. 19-32. Available at: https://doi.org/10.1080/08956308.2010.11657628.

Brown, T. and Katz, B. (no date) Change by design: how design thinking can transform organizations and inspire innovation. Available at: https://onlinelibrary.wiley.com/doi/10.1111/j.1540-5885.2011.00806.x.

Buggie, D, F. (2001) "THE FOUR PHASES OF INNOVATION," Emerald Publishing Limited, 22(5), p. 36-42. Available at: https://doi.org/10.1108/eb040197.

Bunker, K A. (2008, November 1). In focus/responding to change: Helping people manage transition. Wiley, 28(5), 15-17. https://doi.org/10.1002/lia.1263

Burkus, D. (2023, February 6). Inside Adobe's Innovation Kit. https://hbr.org/2015/02/inside-adobes-innovation-kit

Bush, P. (2013) Leadership and Innovation Characteristics. Available at:

sciencedirect.com/science/article/pii/B9780123969934000047.

Case Study Apple Inc. 2008 (2023). Available at:

https://www.slideshare.net/Spartanski/case-study-apple-inc-2008.

Catmull, E. et al. (2015) "From Toy Story to CT Scans: Lessons From Pixar for Radiology," Elsevier BV, 12(9), p. 978-979. Available at: https://doi.org/10.1016/j.jacr.2014.08.010.

Chao, R O., Kavadias, S., & Gaimon, C. (2009, July 11). Revenue Driven Resource Allocation: Funding Authority, Incentives, and New Product Development Portfolio Management. Institute for Operations Research and the Management Sciences, 55(9), 1556-1569. https://doi.org/10.1287/mnsc.1090.1046

Chen, G., Liu, C. and Tjosvold, D. (2005) "Conflict Management for Effective Top Management Teams and Innovation in China*," Wiley, 42(2), p. 277-300. Available at:

https://doi.org/10.1111/j.1467-6486.2005.00497.x.

Cheng, J L C., & Love, E G. (2022, September 16). Designing chief innovation officer positions: a strategic contingency framework. Organizational Design Community, 11(4), 115-128. https://doi.org/10.1007/s41469-022-00126-6

Chopra, S., Flamm, D, S. and Sachin, W. (2017) "Body Scans and Bottlenecks: Optimizing Hospital CT Process Flows," p. 1-6. Available at: https://doi.org/10.1108/case.kellogg.2016.000044.

Chun, Y. and Lee, K. (2013) "Life Cycle-Based Generic Business Strategies for Sustainable Business Models," Canadian Center of Science and Education, 6(8). Available at:

https://doi.org/10.5539/jsd.v6n8p1.

Clemons, E K., & Thatcher, M E. (2008, June 28). Capital One Financial and a decade of experience with newly vulnerable markets: Some propositions concerning the competitive advantage of new entrants. Elsevier BV, 17(3), 179-189.

https://doi.org/10.1016/j.jsis.2008.05.001

Cooper, G, R. (2011) "Perspective: The Innovation Dilemma: How to Innovate When the Market Is Mature," Wiley, 28(s1), p. 2-27. Available at: https://doi.org/10.1111/j.1540-5885.2011.00858.x.

Corrales-Estrada, M. (2019) "Types of Innovation," p. 113-139.

Available at: doi.org/10.1108/978-1-78973-701-120191009.

Crain, C E., Tashima, N., Briody, E K., & McGowan, A R. (2018, June 24). Working at the Speed of Innovation: Impedance Mismatch in Rapid and Innovation Projects. https://doi.org/10.2514/6.2018-4009

Cutler, L. (2000) "Creativity: Essential to Technological Innovation," Taylor & Francis, 43(6), p. 29-30. Available at: https://doi.org/10.1080/08956308.2000.11671391.

Dobni, B, C. (2006) "The innovation blueprint," Elsevier BV, 49(4), p. 329-339. Available at: https://doi.org/10.1016/j.bushor.2005.12.001.

Dobni, C B. (2006, June 1). The innovation blueprint. Elsevier BV, 49(4), 329-339. https://doi.org/10.1016/j.bushor.2005.12.001

Driving cloud adoption in an enterprise IT organization. (2018, September 14). https://learn.microsoft.com/en-us/previous-versions/mt574330(v=technet.10)?redirectedfrom=MSDN

Dubberly, H. (2008) "COVER STORYToward a model of innovation," Association for Computing Machinery, 15(1), p. 28-36. Available at: https://doi.org/10.1145/1330526.1330538.

Eckman, M., Gorski, I. and Mehta, K. (2016) "Leveraging design thinking to build sustainable mobile health systems," Taylor & Francis, 40(7-8), p. 422-430. Available at: https://doi.org/10.1080/03091902.2016.1218560.

Edmondson, A C. (2004, January 1). Psychological Safety, Trust, and Learning in Organizations: A Group-Level Lens.

Edmondson, A C., & Lei, Z. (2014, January 14). Psychological Safety: The History, Renaissance, and Future of an Interpersonal Construct. Annual Reviews, 1(1), 23-43.

https://doi.org/10.1146/annurev-orgpsych-031413-091305

Elmansy, R. (2023) The Double Diamond Design Thinking Process and How to Use it. Available at:

https://www.designorate.com/the-double-diamond-design-thinking-process-and-how-to-use-it/.

Embracing payments as a platform for the future of mobile money. (2023, January 9).

https://www.gsma.com/mobilefordevelopment/wp-content/uploads/2019/02/Embracing-payments-as-a-platform-for-the-future-of-mobile-money.pdf

Employee-Led Innovation. (n.d.).

https://onlinelibrary.wiley.com/doi/10.1111/j.1467-8616.2013.00947.x

Euchner@iriweb.org, J E. (2016, November 5). Building a culture of innovation.

https://www.tandfonline.com/doi/full/10.1080/08956308.2016.1232131

F, f. (1985) Innovation and Entrepreneurship. Available at:

http://ci.nii.ac.jp/ncid/BA78222263.

Fatt, T, P, J. (1998) "Creativity in Business and Innovative Organizations," SAGE Publishing, 12(2), p. 84-92. Available at: https://doi.org/10.1177/095042229801200204.

Fielding high-performing innovation teams. (2019, January 17). https://www.mckinsey.com/capabilities/strategy-and-corporate-finance/our-insights/fielding-high-performing-innovation-teams

Foster an innovative workplace. (2023, February 6). https://rework.withgoogle.com/guides/foster-an-innovative-workplace/steps/introduction/

Framework for Innovation (2024). Available at: https://www.designcouncil.org.uk/our-resources/framework-for-innovation.

Francis, D. and Bessant, J. (2004) "Targeting innovation and implications for capability development," Elsevier BV, 25(3), p. 171-183. Available at: https://doi.org/10.1016/j.technovation.2004.03.004.

Franco, M. and Rodrigues, M. (2019) "Sustainable practices in SMEs: reducing the ecological footprint," Emerald Publishing Limited, 42(2), p. 137-142. Available at: https://doi.org/10.1108/jbs-07-2019-0136.

Garcia, R. (no date) Types of Innovation. Available at: https://onlinelibrary.wiley.com/doi/10.1002/9781118785317.weom130013.

Garcia, R. and Calantone, J, R. (2002) "A critical look at

technological innovation typology and innovativeness terminology: a literature review," Wiley, 19(2), p. 110-132. Available at: https://doi.org/10.1016/s0737-6782(01)00132-1.

Get Started with Design Thinking (2018). Available at: https://dschool.stanford.edu/resources/getting-started-with-design-thinking.

Gilley, A., Dixon, P., & Gilley, J W. (2008, May 30). Characteristics of leadership effectiveness: Implementing change and driving innovation in organizations. Wiley, 19(2), 153-169. https://doi.org/10.1002/hrdq.1232

Glen, R. et al. (2015) "Teaching design thinking in business schools," Elsevier BV, 13(2), p. 182-192. Available at: https://doi.org/10.1016/j.ijme.2015.05.001.

Glen, R., Suciu, C. and Baughn, C, C. (2014) "The Need for Design Thinking in Business Schools," Academy of Management, 13(4), p. 653-667. Available at: https://doi.org/10.5465/amle.2012.0308.

Goldstein, V., & Euchner, J. (2017, October 31). Transformation for Growth at GE. Taylor & Francis, 60(6), 14-19. https://doi.org/10.1080/08956308.2017.1373045

Google's Young, Fun, Productive Corporate Culture (2013). Available at: https://globalyouth.wharton.upenn.edu/articles/googles-young-fun-productive-corporate-culture/.

Guarda, T. et al. (2021) "Digital Transformation Trends and Innovation," IOP Publishing, 1099(1), p. 012062-012062. Available at: https://doi.org/10.1088/1757-899x/1099/1/012062.

Guterl, F. (1984) "Design case history: Apple's Macintosh: A small team of little-known designers, challenged to produce a low-cost, exceptionally easy-to-use personal computer, turns out a technical milestone," Institute of Electrical and Electronics Engineers, 21(12), p. 34-43. Available at:

https://doi.org/10.1109/mspec.1984.6370374.

Higgins, M, J. (1995) "Innovation: The core competence," Emerald Publishing Limited, 23(6), p. 32-36. Available at:

https://doi.org/10.1108/eb054532.

High, P. (2014, November 17). CIO Innovation Budgets Are Increasing.
https://www.forbes.com/sites/peterhigh/2014/11/17/cio-innovation-budgets-are-increasing/

Hisrich, D, R. and Ramadani, V. (2016) "Creativity, Innovation and Entrepreneurial Manager," Springer International Publishing, p. 33-53. Available at:

https://doi.org/10.1007/978-3-319-50467-4_3.

Hornsey, M J., Grice, T., Jetten, J., Paulsen, N., & Callan, V J. (2007, June 9). Group-Directed Criticisms and Recommendations for Change: Why Newcomers Arouse More Resistance Than Old-Timers. SAGE Publishing, 33(7), 1036-1048.

https://doi.org/10.1177/0146167207301029

How GE Appliances Built an Innovation Lab to Rapidly Prototype Products. (2023, February 6).

https://hbr.org/2017/07/how-ge-built-an-innovation-lab-to-rapidly-prototype-appliances

How Pixar Fosters Collective Creativity (2008). Available at:

https://store.hbr.org/product/how-pixar-fosters-collective-creativity/r0809d.

Hunt, D., Lin, A, C. and Atkin, D. (2014) "Photo-messaging: Adopter attributes, technology factors and use motives," Elsevier BV, 40, p. 171-179. Available at:

https://doi.org/10.1016/j.chb.2014.07.030.

IDEO Design thinking process | RNF Technologies (2020). Available at: https://www.rnftechnologies.com/blog/design-thinking-steps/ideo-design-thinking-process.

ISO. (2022) ISO 56002:2019 - Innovation management system 2022. Available at:

https://www.iso.org/files/live/sites/isoorg/files/store/en/PUB1004 68.pdf.

Ingram, N. (2018) "Tesla Motors: A Potentially Disruptive Force in a Mature Industry," 5(1), p. 8-22. Available at:

https://doi.org/10.18646/2056.51.18-002.

InnovatingSociety (2020) Doblin – 10 types of Innovation. Available at: https://innovatingsociety.com/doblin-10-types-of-innovation/.

Innovation management — Innovation management system — Guidance (2024). Available at: https://www.iso.org/standard/68221.html.

Ireland, D, R. and Hitt, A, M. (2005) "Achieving and maintaining strategic competitiveness in the 21st century: The role of strategic leadership," Academy of Management, 19(4), p. 63-77. Available at: https://doi.org/10.5465/ame.2005.19417908.

Islam, N. and Want, R. (2014) "Smartphones: Past, Present, and Future," Institute of Electrical and Electronics Engineers, 13(4), p. 89-92. Available at: https://doi.org/10.1109/mprv.2014.74.

Jensen Huang NTU Commencement Speech 2023 (2023). Available at: https://interconnected.blog/jensen-huang-ntu-commencement-speech-2023/.

Jensen, R. (1999) "The fifth society – and its successful businesses," Emerald Publishing Limited, 1(3), p. 213-216. Available at: https://doi.org/10.1108/14636689910802142.

Johnston, E, R. and Kaplan, S. (1996) "Harnessing the Power of Strategic Innovation," Wiley, 5(2), p. 117-121. Available at: https://doi.org/10.1111/j.1467-8691.1996.tb00130.x.

Jonash, S, R. (2005) "Driving sustainable growth and innovation: pathways to high performance leadership," 6(1), p. 197-202. Available at: https://doi.org/10.1108/08944310510557468.

Jones, N, J., Cope, J. and Kintz, A. (2016) "Peering into the Future of Innovation Management," Taylor & Francis, 59(4), p. 49-58. Available at: https://doi.org/10.1080/08956308.2016.1185344.

Jones, W, R. (2023) NVIDIA CEO Jensen Huang Reveals Keys to AI and Leadership. Available at:

https://leading.business.columbia.edu/main-pillar-digital-future/digital-future/ai-nvidia-ceo-jensen-huang.

Juliana, O, N. et al. (2021) "The Impact of Creativity and Innovation on Entrepreneurship Development: Evidence from Nigeria," Scientific Research Publishing, 09(04), p. 1743-1770. Available at: https://doi.org/10.4236/ojbm.2021.94095.

Kadar, M., Moise, A, I. and Colomba, C. (2014) "Innovation Management in the Globalized Digital Society," Elsevier BV, 143, p. 1083-1089. Available at:

https://doi.org/10.1016/j.sbspro.2014.07.560.

Kadar, M., Moise, I A., & Colomba, C. (2014, August 1). Innovation Management in the Globalized Digital Society. Elsevier BV, 143, 1083-1089.

https://doi.org/10.1016/j.sbspro.2014.07.560

Kev.desouza@gmail.com, K C D U O W. (n.d). Overcoming Technology Resistance.

https://onlinelibrary.wiley.com/doi/10.1111/j.1467-8616.2007.00495.x

Khaire, M, a, A, M, T, b. (2014) Creativity and the Role of the Leader. Available at: https://hbr.org/2008/10/creativity-and-the-role-of-the-leader.

Kline, J, S. and Rosenberg, N. (2009) "An Overview of Innovation," p. 173-203. Available at: https://ideas.repec.org/h/wsi/wschap/9789814273596_0009.html.

Kriegesmann, B., Kley, T., & Schwering, M G. (2007, May 22). Making organizational learning happen: the value of "creative failures," 8(4), 270-276. https://doi.org/10.1108/17515630710684312

Kylliäinen, J. (2023) "Types of Innovation – The Ultimate Guide with Definitions and Examples," HYPE Innovation, 4 May. Available at: https://www.viima.com/blog/types-of-innovation.

Loewe, P. and Dominiquini, J. (2006) "Overcoming the barriers to effective innovation," Emerald Publishing Limited, 34(1), p. 24-31. Available at: https://doi.org/10.1108/10878570610637858.

Loewe, P. and Dominiquini, J. (2006) "Overcoming the barriers to effective innovation," Emerald Publishing Limited, 34(1), p. 24-31. Available at: https://doi.org/10.1108/10878570610637858.

Lorenz, C, R. (2010) "What is innovation?: Insights and perspectives on the term 'innovation'," Inderscience Publishers, 6(1), p. 63-63. Available at: https://doi.org/10.1504/ijtip.2010.033924.

Lowry, O. et al. (1951) "Protein Measurement With The Folin Phenol Reagent," Elsevier BV, 193(1), p. 265-275. Available at: https://doi.org/10.1016/s0021-9258(19)52451-6.

Luzinski, C. (2014) "Identifying Leadership Competencies of the Future: Introducing the Use of Strategic Foresight," Elsevier BV, 12(4), p. 37-47. Available at: https://doi.org/10.1016/j.mnl.2014.05.009.

Making innovation structures work. (2012, September 1). https://www.mckinsey.com/capabilities/strategy-and-corporate-finance/our-insights/making-innovation-structures-work-mckinsey-global-survey-results

Managing Your Innovation Portfolio (2023). Available at: https://hbr.org/2012/05/managing-your-innovation-portfolio.

Mars, M, M. (2013) "Framing the Conceptual Meaning and Fundamental Principles of Innovation," p. 1-12. Available at: https://doi.org/10.1108/s1048-4736(2013)0000023003.

McGrady, E. et al. (2010) "Emerging Technologies in Healthcare: Navigating Risks, Evaluating Rewards," Lippincott Williams & Wilkins, 55(5), p. 353-365. Available at: https://doi.org/10.1097/00115514-201009000-00011.

McMillan, C. (2009) "Five competitive forces of effective leadership and innovation," Emerald Publishing Limited, 31(1), p. 11-22. Available at: https://doi.org/10.1108/02756661011012741.

Meskó, B. (2017) "The role of artificial intelligence in precision medicine," Taylor & Francis, 2(5), p. 239-241. Available at: https://doi.org/10.1080/23808993.2017.1380516.

Morrison, L, J. (2013) "A Review of 'Leaders Make the Future:

Ten New Leadership Skills for an Uncertain World'," Taylor & Francis, 89(1), p. 57-58. Available at:

https://doi.org/10.1080/08832323.2012.731438.

Musk, R, E. (2017) "Making Humans a Multi-Planetary Species," Mary Ann Liebert, Inc., 5(2), p. 46-61. Available at:

https://doi.org/10.1089/space.2017.29009.emu.

NVIDIA – Inventor of the GPU (2023). Available at:

https://www.slideshare.net/NVIDIA/nvidia-the-ai-company.

Narayanan, V K. (2017, January 16). Idea labs: instituting an innovation discovery process capable of sustaining the business. Emerald Publishing Limited, 45(1), 27-36.

https://doi.org/10.1108/sl-12-2016-0089

Oe, H., Yamaoka, Y. and Duda, K. (2022) "How to Sustain Businesses in the Post-COVID-19 Era: A Focus on Innovation, Sustainability and Leadership," Sumy State University, 6(4), p. 1-9. Available at: https://doi.org/10.21272/bel.6(4).1-9.2022.

Ottinger, R. (2024) Create Sustainable Success with the 4 Types of Innovation. Available at:

https://www.freshconsulting.com/insights/blog/the-4-types-of-innovation/.

O'Regan, N. (2012) "Entrepreneurship and innovation: Overview," Wiley, 21(5-6), p. 193-198. Available at:

https://doi.org/10.1002/jsc.1903.

Pachava, V. (2018) "Innovation and Competitiveness – Small and

Medium Enterprises in India," 5(1(4)), p. 115-115. Available at: https://doi.org/10.18843/ijms/v5i1(4)/18.

Pangarkar, N. (2015) "Performance implications of strategic changes: An integrative framework," Elsevier BV, 58(3), p. 295-304. Available at: https://doi.org/10.1016/j.bushor.2015.01.003.

Posner, Z, B. and Kouzes, M, J. (1996) "Ten Lessons for Leaders and Leadership Developers," SAGE Publishing, 3(3), p. 3-10. Available at: https://doi.org/10.1177/107179199700300302.

Prather, C W. (2008, March 1). Use Mistakes to Foster Innovation. Taylor & Francis, 51(2), 14-16.

https://doi.org/10.1080/08956308.2008.11657490

Principles of Social Psychology. (2015, October 27). https://open.lib.umn.edu/socialpsychology/chapter/7-5-chapter-summary/

Ram, S., & Sheth, J N. (1989, February 1). Consumer Resistance to Innovations: The Marketing Problem and its solutions. Emerald Publishing Limited, 6(2), 5-14.

https://doi.org/10.1108/eum0000000002542

Reid, S., Roberts, D. and Moore, K. (2014) "Technology Vision for Radical Innovation and Its Impact on Early Success," Wiley, 32(4), p. 593-609. Available at:

https://doi.org/10.1111/jpim.12221.

Reiner, I, B. (2008) "Intellectual Property in Medical Imaging and Informatics: The Independent Inventor's Perspective," Springer

Science+Business Media, 21(1), p. 3-8. Available at: https://doi.org/10.1007/s10278-007-9096-6.

Roth, W. and Capuano, T. (2001) "Systemic versus Nonsystemic Approaches To Quality Improvement," Wiley, 20(2), p. 57-64. Available at: https://doi.org/10.1002/npr.2027.

Rowe, G, P. (1987) Design Thinking. Available at: https://www.amazon.com/Design-Thinking-Press-Peter-Rowe/dp/026268067X.

Ruffles, C, P. (2000) "Improving the new product introduction process in manufacturing companies," Inderscience Publishers, 1(1),p. 1-1. Available at: https://doi.org/10.1504/ijmtm.2000.001332.

Sage, P, A. (1995) "Systems engineering and systems management for reengineering," Elsevier BV, 30(1-2), p. 3-25. Available at: https://doi.org/10.1016/0164-1212(94)00114-3.

Sarkees, M. and Hulland, J. (2008) "Innovation and efficiency: It is possible to have it all," Elsevier BV, 52(1), p. 45-55. Available at: https://doi.org/10.1016/j.bushor.2008.08.002.

Schilling, A, M. (2004) Strategic Management of Technological Innovation. Available at: http://www.gbv.de/dms/zbw/605130337.pdf.

Schmitt, R. and Almeida, F. (2020) "Building a culture of continuous innovation: How Pixar and Google address this challenge?" p. 22-39. Available at:

https://doi.org/10.31039/jomeino.2020.4.1.2.

Seedhouse, E. (2013) "Elon Musk: The space industry's Tony Stark," Springer Nature, p. 1-15. Available at: https://doi.org/10.1007/978-1-4614-5514-1_1.

Shao, X., Wang, Q. and Yang, H. (2021) Business Analysis and Future Development of an Electric Vehicle Company-Tesla. Available at: https://doi.org/10.2991/assehr.k.211020.188.

Shih, C, W. and Kaufman, P, S. (2014) Netflix in 2011. Available at: https://www.hbs.edu/faculty/Pages/item.aspx?num=47834.

Shy, O. (2012, January 2). Account-to-Account Electronic Money Transfers: Recent Developments in the United States. De Gruyter, 11(1). https://doi.org/10.1515/1446-9022.1297

Silva, I S., Bernardes, P., Ramalho, F D., Ekel, P., Martins, C A P D S., & Libório, M P. (2019, September 19). Continuous results-driven innovation management program. Emerald Publishing Limited, 26(4), 389-408.

https://doi.org/10.1108/rege-01-2019-0006

Sinha, N., Kakkar, N. and Gupta, V. (2009) "Unleash the power of creativity and innovation," 1(4), p. 417-417. Available at: https://doi.org/10.1504/ijssm.2009.030515.

Sinha, N., Kakkar, N. and Gupta, V. (2009) "Unleash the power of creativity and innovation," 1(4), p. 417-417. Available at: https://doi.org/10.1504/ijssm.2009.030515.

Sivakumar, K. and Feng, C. (2019) "Patterns of product

improvements and customer response," Elsevier BV, 104, p. 27-43. Available at: https://doi.org/10.1016/j.jbusres.2019.06.044.

Smith, K, W. (2014) "Dynamic Decision Making: A Model of Senior Leaders Managing Strategic Paradoxes," Academy of Management, 57(6), p. 1592-1623. Available at: https://doi.org/10.5465/amj.2011.0932.

Soken, N. and Barnes, K, B. (2014) "What kills innovation? Your role as a leader in supporting an innovative culture," Emerald Publishing Limited, 46(1), p. 7-15. Available at: https://doi.org/10.1108/ict-09-2013-0057.

Soken, N. and Barnes, K, B. (2014) "What kills innovation? Your role as a leader in supporting an innovative culture," Emerald Publishing Limited, 46(1), p. 7-15. Available at: https://doi.org/10.1108/ict-09-2013-0057.

Soken, N. and Barnes, K, B. (2014) "What kills innovation? Your role as a leader in supporting an innovative culture," Emerald Publishing Limited, 46(1), p. 7-15. Available at: https://doi.org/10.1108/ict-09-2013-0057.

Soken, N., & Barnes, B K. (2014, January 28). What kills innovation? Your role as a leader in supporting an innovative culture. Emerald Publishing Limited, 46(1), 7-15. https://doi.org/10.1108/ict-09-2013-0057

Soken, N., & Barnes, B K. (2014, January 28). What kills innovation? Your role as a leader in supporting an innovative culture. Emerald Publishing Limited, 46(1), 7-15.

https://doi.org/10.1108/ict-09-2013-0057

Stamm, v, B. (2009) "Leadership for innovation: what you can do to create a culture conducive to innovation," Emerald Publishing Limited, 25(6), p. 13-15. Available at:

https://doi.org/10.1108/02580540910952154.

Stevens, W, C. (2011) "Using transformational leadership to guide an organization's success," Wiley, 37(4), p. 37-44. Available at:

https://doi.org/10.1002/ert.20319.

Stone, B, b. (2015) Twitter's Cofounder on Creating Opportunities ^ R1506A. Available at:

https://store.hbr.org/product/twitter-s-cofounder-on-creating-opportunities/r1506a?sku=R1506A-PDF-ENG.

Striffolino, P. and Saunders, A, S. (1989) "Emerging Leaders," Taylor & Francis, 27(1), p. 51-58. Available at:

https://doi.org/10.1080/00220973.1989.11072134.

Suran, S. (2002, December 23). How to implement change effectively. Wiley, 14(2), 31-38.

https://doi.org/10.1002/jcaf.10134

Ten Types of Innovation (2023). Available at:

https://www.deloittedigital.com/us/en/offerings/customer-led-marketing/customer-strategy-and-applied-design/applied-design-and-innovation/ten-types.html.

The 5 Myths of Innovation (2010). Available at:

https://sloanreview.mit.edu/article/the-5-myths-of-innovation/.

The Double Diamond: Strategy + Execution of the Right Solution (2015). Available at:

https://www.thoughtworks.com/insights/blog/double-diamond.

The Invention of the Post-it® Note. (2024, June 14).

https://www.invent.org/blog/trends-stem/who-invented-post-it-notes

The Pixar Way: 37 Quotes on Developing and Maintaining a Creative Company (2023). Available at:

https://www.slideshare.net/Bplans/the-pixar-way-37-quotes.

The Role of the CIO-Enabler and Visionary. (n.d).

https://onlinelibrary.wiley.com/doi/10.1002/9781119201434.ch11

The Sprint Book (2024). Available at:

https://www.thesprintbook.com/.

The design sprint (no date). Available at:

https://www.thesprintbook.com/the-design-sprint.

The excellent culture of Pixar (2023). Available at:

https://www.slideshare.net/MatthewHuff8/the-excellent-culture-of-pixar-66547520.

The rise of digital remittances: How innovation is improving global money movement. (2021, April 5).

https://usa.visa.com/content/dam/VCOM/global/ms/documents/veei-the-rise-of-digital-remittances.pdf

The title is "What is Innovation." (no date). Available at:

https://onlinelibrary.wiley.com/doi/10.1002/9781118386781.ch2.

Tirmizi, A, M, S., Malik, A, Q. and Hussain, S, S. (2020) "Invention and Open Innovation Processes, and Linkages: A Conceptual Framework," Springer Science+Business Media, 6(4), p. 159-159. Available at:

https://doi.org/10.3390/joitmc6040159.

Topalian, A. (2000) "The Role of Innovation Leaders in Developing Long-Term Products," Imperial College Press, 4(2), p. 149-171. Available at:

https://doi.org/10.1016/s1363-9196(00)00009-3.

Tucker, B, R. (2001) "Innovation," Emerald Publishing Limited, 29(1),p. 11-14. Available at:

https://doi.org/10.1108/10878570110694616.

Twilk@cmu.edu, P, 1, P, U, M, C, W, R, T. (2018) The "I" in Team: How Developing Individual Strength, Builds a Great Team. Available at: https://dl.acm.org/doi/10.1145/3235715.3235730.

Types of Innovation (no date). Available at:

https://papers.ssrn.com/sol3/papers.cfm?abstract_id=2262206.

Varadarajan, R. (2008) "Fortune at the bottom of the innovation pyramid: The strategic logic of incremental innovations," Elsevier BV, 52(1),p. 21-29. Available at:

https://doi.org/10.1016/j.bushor.2008.03.011.

Varadarajan, R. (2018) "Innovation, Innovation Strategy, and Strategic Innovation," Emerald Publishing Limited, p. 143-166.

Available at: https://doi.org/10.1108/s1548-643520180000015007

Vetter, S. (2024) Corporate innovation: Team Setup, Budgeting Strategies and Return On Investment (ROI). Available at: https://www.innovate-strategy.com/articles/corporate-innovation-team-setup.

Walton, T. (2002) "Establishing a culture of creativity," Wiley, 13(2), p. 6-9. Available at: https://doi.org/10.1111/j.1948-7169.2002.tb00302.x.

Wang, Y, K. and Casimir, G. (2007) "How Attitudes of Leaders May Enhance Organizational Creativity: Evidence from a Chinese Study," Wiley, 16(3), p. 229-238. Available at:

https://doi.org/10.1111/j.1467-8691.2007.00443.x.

What Kind of Chief Innovation Officer Does Your Company Need? (2023, February 6). https://hbr.org/2019/11/what-kind-of-chief-innovation-officer-does-your-company-need

Why, What, and How of Management Innovation (2006). Available at: https://store.hbr.org/product/why-what-and-how-of-management-innovation/r0602c.

Yin, Z, J. (1994) "Managing process innovation through incremental improvements: Empirical evidence in the petroleum refining industry," Elsevier BV, 47(3),p. 265-276. Available at:

https://doi.org/10.1016/0040-1625(94)90068-x.

Yu, O. (2017, July 1). Innovation Management: A Need-Centered Optimal Joint Investment Approach, 7, 1-12.

https://doi.org/10.23919/picmet.2017.8125358

Yukl, G. and Lepsinger, R. (2006) "Leading change: Adapting and innovating in an uncertain world," Wiley, 26(2), p. 3-7. Available at: https://doi.org/10.1002/lia.1154.

Zhang, N. and Lee, G. (2016) Consumer valuations on digital product innovation. Available at:

https://doi.org/10.1145/2971603.2971642

Şimşit, T, Z., Vayvay, Ö. and Öztürk, Ö. (2014) "An Outline of Innovation Management Process: Building a Framework for Managers to Implement Innovation," Elsevier BV, 150, p. 690-699. Available at: https://doi.org/10.1016/j.sbspro.2014.09.021.

About the Author

Ugeng Wijaya is a globally recognised thought leader in Agile and Innovation, ranked among the Top 25 by Thinkers360. Over the past decade, he has helped more than 50 organisations across the Asia Pacific embrace change and drive transformation. As the founder and director of the Board of Transformation and Excellence (BTX), Wijaya leads a consulting powerhouse specialising in business innovation and digital transformation. With an MSc in innovation management & entrepreneurship from the University of Manchester, UK, Wijaya brings a rare blend of academic insight and real-world experience to the table. Known for his provocative, game-changing approach, he empowers leaders to redefine possibilities and adapt to the relentless pace of change.

www.ingramcontent.com/pod-product-compliance
Lightning Source LLC
Chambersburg PA
CBHW061733120626
46550CB00005B/1787